# Donald Featherstone's Wargaming Pike and Shot

**Revised Edition**

**Edited by John Curry**

This book was first published in 1977 as *Wargaming Pike-and-Shot* by David & Charles Ltd. The original book has been supplemented by an unpublished set of rules by Donald Featherstone contained in his archive. Some notes have been added, together with suggestions for further reading.

This edition printed 2010
Copyright © 2010 John Curry and Donald Featherstone
With thanks to Arthur Harman for his assistance in the preparation of this volume.

All rights reserved. No part of this book may be reproduced or transmitted in any form by any means, electronic, mechanical, photocopying, recording, or otherwise without the prior written permission of the authors.

Books edited by John Curry as part of the History of Wargaming Project
*Army Wargames: Staff College Exercises 1870-1980.*
*Charlie Wesencraft's Practical Wargaming*
*Charlie Wesencraft's With Pike and Musket*
*Donald Featherstone's War Games*
*Donald Featherstone's Skirmish Wargaming*
*Donald Featherstone's Naval Wargames*
*Donald Featherstone's Advanced Wargames*
*Donald Featherstone's Wargaming Campaigns*
*Donald Featherstone's Solo Wargaming*
*Donald Featherstone's Wargaming Airborne Operations*
*Donald Featherstone's Lost Tales*
*The Fred Jane Naval Wargame (1906) including the Royal Navy War Game (1921)*
*Paddy Griffith's Napoleonic Wargaming for Fun*
*Sprawling Wargames: Multi-player wargaming by Paddy Griffith*
*Verdy's 'Free Kriegspiel' including the Victorian Army's 1896 War Game*
*Tony Bath's Ancient Wargaming*
*Phil Dunn's Sea Battles*
*Peter Perla's The Art of Wargaming*
*Phil Barkers Introduction to Ancient Warfare and 6th Edition Ancients*
and many others

See The History of Wargaming Project at www.wargaming.co for a continually expanding range of wargaming publications.

ISBN 978-1-4466-3747-0

Foreword on Donald Featherstone's Wargaming Pike and Shot Revised Edition    5

Introduction    7

1. The Battle of Ravenna 11 April 1512    14

2. The Battle of Pavia 24 February 1525    20

3. The Battle of Mohacs 29 August 1526    27

4. The Battle of Ceresole 14 April 1544    33

5. The Battle of Pinkie 10 September 1547    39

6. The Battle of Dreux 19 December 1562    45

7. The Battle of Coutras 20 October 1587    52

8. The Battle of Arques 21 September 1589    59

9. The Battle of Nieuport 2 July 1600    66

10. The Battle of Breitenfeld 18 September 1631    75

11. The Battle of Lützen 16 November 1632    83

12. The Battle of Rocroi 19 May 1643    91

13. The Battle of Cropredy Bridge 29 June 1644    97

14. The Battle of Auldearn 9 May 1645    103

15. The Battle of the Dunes (Dunkirk) 14 June 1658    109

16. English Civil War Rules by Donald Featherstone    115

Appendix 1 Rules for Wargames    119

Appendix 2 Availability of Wargames Figures    123

Appendix 3 Terrain    127

Bibliography    129

# Foreword on Donald Featherstone's Wargaming Pike and Shot Revised Edition

A general in this era had two main aims. His first was to disrupt the enemy line of battle; his second was then to destroy the enemy army that had lost its cohesion. He also had the aim of capturing the enemy artillery train and the potential to capture the even greater prize, the baggage train.

It was often considered good practice to deploy for an engagement in three lines: The first was to engage the enemy, the second to provide support and the third to act as a reserve. A 'chessboard' type deployment, with gaps between units, permitted units from rearward lines to move through and allowed individuals from routed units to flow through the battle line without disrupting it. Units of cavalry and infantry were often alternated to provide mutual support. Protecting the flanks was seen as essential. Pinning flanks on difficult terrain or using cavalry to screen the flanks were favoured tactics. Small parties of musketeers were detached to be skirmishers, for reconnaissance across difficult terrain or to support units of cavalry by their weight of fire.

Battles often started with a relatively ineffective artillery barrage. It was usually considered best to attack first to gain the initiative. Cavalry were often seen as having the greater shock effect and their relative speed could surprise the enemy line.

Leadership was important and the army commander had two choices. Leading from the front, like Gustavus Adolphus, could provide inspiration to the soldiers and could allow the general to react immediately to events in the battle, but it had its risks. Staying back helped a commander's control of the general battle and increased his life expectancy, but it also increased the time to react to the flow of battle. It was normal to have different commanders for the left, right, centre and reserve.

Armies of this era were starting to develop flexibility. At Breitenfeld, the Imperial and Swedish commanders moved their cavalry across the entire battlefield to strike at the enemy's flank and rear. During the Thirty Years' War, the Swedish army developed light artillery which allowed guns to take the offensive by keeping up with the advancing infantry formations.

In Chapter 8 of *Wargames Campaigns*[1], Don Featherstone described the English Civil War as 'A colourful period that has much to

---

[1] First published by Stanley Paul, 1970; now republished in The History of Wargaming Project.

offer the wargamer, for some inexplicable reason it has not been explored in a wargaming sense!'[2]

Ironically, Brigadier Peter Young, early wargamer, distinguished soldier and military historian, author of several highly-regarded books on the English Civil War[3] and founder and first Captain-Generall of the Sealed Knot re-enactment society[4]- which could almost be regarded as skirmish wargaming with real people, rather than toy soldiers! – chose, instead, the 'Lace Wars' of the eighteenth century for his classic wargame book *Charge: or, How to play war games*[5].

To Don Featherstone, therefore, fell the task of raising the profile of the 'Pike and Shot' period in the minds of wargamers, and this book was one way in which he did so.

Historical research – much of it by wargamers and re-enactors – has led to far greater knowledge and understanding of the campaigns, tactics and equipment of the armies described in these pages than was the case when this book was first written, but Don's practical advice on how to wargame the battles remains just as stimulating and inspiring.

The wide variety of figures and rules available for the period today, examples of which are listed in the appendices, show just how successful he was in helping to establish 'Pike and Shot' as the major wargaming period it is today.

This classic book is a combination of military history and the wargame. Don aimed to provide the reader with sufficient information to allow a recreation of a particular battle, not just as an entertaining wargame, but as a tool to explore the one of the great mysteries of all time, the tactical details of an historical battle. Recreating these key battles offers an insight into the developing tactics of the Pike of and Shot era. Let battle commence.

John Curry, Editor of the History of Wargaming Project

www.wargaming.co

.

---

[2] The only other wargame book on the period was *With Pike and Musket; Sixteenth and Seventeenth Century Battles for the Wargamer,* C. F. Wesencraft, The Elmfield Press, 1975; now republished in The History of Wargaming Project.

[3] *Edgehill 1642; The Campaign and the Battle,* Kineton 1967; *Marston Moor 1644,* Kineton, 1970; *Naseby 1645: The Campaign and the Battle*, Century, 1985; *The English Civil War* (with Richard Holmes) 1974; *Sieges of the Great Civil War,* (with Wilf Emberton), London, 1978.

[4] *Commando to Captain-Generall: the life of Brigadier Peter Young,* Alison Mitchell, Pen & Sword Books, 2007; www.thesealedknot.org.uk.

[5] Co-author Lt.-Col. J.P. Lawford, Morgan-Grampian,1967; paperback reprint 1986.

# Introduction

IN THE EARLY FIFTEENTH CENTURY artillery and the handheld firearm were rapidly superseding the bow and edged weapons, and for the next 250 years 'pike-and-shot' prevailed. Gunpowder so dominated the battlefield that armour, except for the helmet and breastplate worn by heavy cavalry and pikemen, was discarded[6]. It was an era that had many positive forward steps in the art of warfare and is particularly attractive for simulation in miniature because of its colour and brilliant commanders; it is packed with tactical innovations, and many of its battles were fought in compact areas with small numbers of men arriving on the battlefield because of the difficulties of travelling on the few bad roads that were available, and because of an often less than perfect intelligence system, the need to protect communications, and the chronic financial troubles that made it hard even to pay national troops, let alone hire mercenaries. The days of the massed levy had yet to come, and cash was often the controlling factor over the size of an army.

Many of the fifteenth, sixteenth and early seventeenth century battles were worthy of reproduction being coloured by highly competent soldiers — Henry of Navarre, Gustavus Adolphus, the young Enghien (later to become the great Conde), Montrose, Maurice of Orange, and Turenne. In addition, all the battles described in this book possess tactical and human aspects that make them attractive to simulate.

In practically every battle reconstruction herein the actual numbers of men can be conveniently ignored, provided that there is a body of troops on the wargames table corresponding to each formation taking part in the battle. Thus, at Cropredy Bridge, Waller put into the field three bodies of cavalry totalling about 2,500 troopers and about the same number of infantry, a force that, with any conventional scaling down, requires a fair number of figures. But they can be represented by three bodies of cavalry of any number to simulate the forces of Middleton, Hazlerig and Vandruske, and four separate bodies of foot soldiers to represent the 18 companies of Parliamentary infantry that took part in the early stages of the battle. As these infantry were chased off the field, the same Figures can be used to represent the Kentish and the Tower Hamlet Regiments, so successful in the latter part of the engagement. In those battles where only part of an army was engaged, or its separate parts engaged at varying times, the same group of figures can be used more than once, so drastically reducing the numbers required for the battle.

---

[6] Though later wars did periodically see the use of body armour for specialists, such as for snipers. Modern soldiers see body armour as an indispensible part of their equipment.

Reconstructing a battle as a wargame is less a demonstration than a competitive exercise, presenting the challenge of reversing the result by the introduction of interesting tactical developments. For the reconstruction to bear more than a titular resemblance to the battle itself, the table-top terrain must closely resemble, both in scale and appearance, the area of the original conflict, and the number of formations must conform to those historically present. It is not enough, however, to construct a terrain resembling that of Auldearn, for example, and allow numerous painted miniatures of infantry, cavalry and artillery, to disport themselves in a way that bears only the vaguest resemblance to the original conflict. The battle has to be considered in its correct chronological context if its reconstruction is to present an authentic simulation, within the limits of suggested Military Possibilities. If it is controlled so as to allow the historical formations to follow the tactical plans, use the weapons and fight in the manner of their day, the table-top encounter may well follow its historical course. But if unrealistic rules control the reconstruction, or if a knowledgeable wargamer is permitted to manoeuvre his armies with a tactical hindsight denied to the real-life commander, the wargame will bear little relation to reality.

The table-top miniature Scots army of the Regent Arran at Pinkie in 1547 for instance, must not be allowed to ford the River Esk and attack with the discipline and steadiness of the Guards at the Alma, for that would allow the battle to degenerate into a farce. It must be accepted that the tactics and the manner of fighting of all armies conform to their known and recorded style at the battle under review. This is difficult to achieve because it is not easy for a wargamer to eradicate all knowledge of modern military tactics, and the wargamer handling the losing side may be disinclined slavishly to follow a course of action so obviously doomed to failure. To prevent possible anomalies, details are provided herein of the type of troops and their style of fighting, so that the wargamer can manoeuvre them in an historically correct manner.

The rest of the Introduction concerns the specific factors that control the authentic reconstruction of the battles described in this book.

**Classification of Commanders**
If both forces are equal in strength, morale, equipment, position, mobility etc, on the wargames table or in real warfare, victory will go to the side with the best commander. On those occasions in this book when a force was defeated by a numerically weaker army, as at Auldearn, it was generally because the commander of the weaker side possessed outstanding tactical ability and could inspire his men to exceptional heights. Failing that, he may just have been the better commander on the day. When wargaming, the ability of a commander is more or less that of the wargamer representing him, but this factor is balanced by giving those leaders who were historically superior an 'above average' classification, whereas known incompetents are classified 'below average'.

On the wargames table the troops of an 'above average' commander display higher morale and better fighting qualities than those unfortunates led by an 'average' or 'below average' commander. This differentiation is achieved by adding or subtracting from the dice scores that control morale and fighting ability. For instance, troops led by an 'above average' commander add, say, 1 to their dice, troops under a 'below average' commander deduct 1, and those men led by an 'average' commander do not alter their dice scores.

An 'above average' commander, by being allowed to be 'himself', is granted greater flexibility of movement and, within certain limits, can employ tactics of another period and issue fresh orders at the start of each game-move; the 'below average' commander is compelled to manoeuvre and control his army strictly in conformation with its known style of fighting, and his troops must stick rigidly to their initial orders until they are disorganised by some forced reaction, such as a disastrous morale rating. The 'average' commander is allowed, within certain limits, to alter characteristic fighting patterns while controlling and manoeuvring his force in accordance with its known style of fighting, and is permitted to change his orders every third game-move.

An interesting (and sometimes amusing) method of simulating the classification of commanders is to bestow the mantle of the 'below average' commander upon novice wargamers and that of the 'above average' commander on an experienced or veteran wargamer. Sometimes subordinate commanders merit higher ratings than their leaders, as at Cropredy Bridge, where, in the later stages of the battle, Colonel Baines undoubtedly displayed far more courage and tactical sense than did Waller, his commander.

**Morale**
Morale concerns the confidence and the individual and collective discipline of soldiers. It is the intangible factor that causes a body of troops suddenly to break and run, or to rally and fight 'above themselves'. Inevitably, the morale rules used in wargames of any period bear a basic resemblance to each other, because the factors that frighten or stimulate soldiers have not really changed since the beginnings of time, though they are much affected by such variables as confidence in a commander, high standards of training and discipline, and battle experience.

Military history reveals many occasions when smaller forces were victorious because their morale was higher than that of their opponents. On the wargames table careful manipulation of the comparative morale status of opposing troops makes possible battles between forces with marked numerical disparities. Arques, fought on 21 September 1589, requires balancing in this manner.

With the possible exception of the Saxon allies of the Swedes at Breitenfeld, there was no occasion in any of the fifteen battles under review when one side entered the arena in a markedly lower state of morale than their opponents. Conversely, the eventual outcome of almost every one of these battles is strictly related to the progressive raising of the morale of the winning side and the equivalent lowering of that of the losers.

Morale factors feature prominently in the rules that control table-top wargames. The little mindless lead or plastic figures need to have intelligence and emotion bestowed upon them, to accord with specific times and circumstances. This can be reflected by troops starting the battle with an 'average' state of morale which, according to the fluctuations of combat, will rise or fall. For example, if the average morale status of a unit is represented by the figure 6, 1 may be added for the support of a friendly unit on flanks or rear, and another 1 if the Commander-in-Chief is with them, making a total of 8. You may deduct 1 from that total if the unit loses a quarter of its men, another 1 if they come under artillery fire, 1 more if they have to move back, and 2 if, in the last game-move, they lose a melee -- leaving a final total of 3. Then a die is thrown to represent those fluctuations of fortune that are an inevitable adjunct to war. If the score is 3, this figure, added to the original 3, indicates that the unit has maintained its morale value of 6 and is still in first-class shape. If the die score is 2, then the unit's morale will fall below par, causing it to withdraw; and a die throw of 1 will reduce the unit's morale to such a state that it may well run away from the field.

**Surprise**
With wargamers towering in godlike fashion over their table-top battlefield, the factor of surprise is most difficult to simulate, yet the recurring presence of this factor in warfare means that it must be represented if battles are to be accurately reconstructed. Of the battles described in this book, the element of surprise was present at Pavia in 1525; to a lesser extent at Pinkie in 1547; in the unexpected encounter at Dreux in 1562; possibly (because of the fog) at Lutzen in 1632; partially in Waller's sudden attack on the rearguard at Cropredy Bridge, and, more strongly than in any other battle described, at Auldearn.

The surprise that enabled Montrose's horse, under Gordon and Aboyne, to fling themselves upon the flank of the unsuspecting enemy at Auldearn could be extremely difficult to simulate on the wargames table. On this particular occasion the layout of the terrain enables the element of surprise to be achieved by the simplest of means — with the outflanking force considered to be exactly on the baseline, just off the table, so that it is a simple matter to measure from the edge of the table when they commence their flanking charge. Even so, the handling of Montrose's flanking force needs to be carefully controlled if it is to be realistic and not to infuriate the astonished wargamer taking the part of Hurry. The relative absence of strong surprise factors in the battles under discussion make it unnecessary to go into lengthy details as to means of its simulation; also it has been considered at some depth in the first of the two volumes in the series *Battle Notes for Wargamers*[7].

Without exception, each battle described herein will be better simulated by both 'commanders' being unaware of the name of the battle they are fighting or of its tactical details. Both could be presented by a narrative that sets the scene and no more, or the 'host' wargamer might arrange for his guest to take the part of the 'surprised' commander — and be ready to placate him afterwards!

The simulation of a commander's reaction to a surprise move can reflect his above-normal ability by such ploys as that made in the wargame reconstruction of the Battle of Pinkie. Here Somerset, the English commander, takes one-third of a game-move to react to the Regent Arran's surprise assault, and is then given a brief note of the tactics employed by his namesake in the battle itself. Of course, he is under no compulsion to follow this historical course of action, but, as it was successful and probably the best tactics for the occasion, the table-top Somerset may do well to conform to it.

**Chance Cards**

Closely akin to Military Possibilities, Chance Cards prescribe unexpected events that, by introducing pleasant and/or unpleasant factors, can materially affect the course or even the outcome of a battle. Their worded instructions pose mental, physical and tactical eventualities that require compliance by the commander drawing the card. They are useful, for example, when a wargamer needs to know whether a courier has arrived, and at what time, for they will state whether or not the man has been delayed (perhaps by guerrilla attack), or if his thoroughbred horse has brought him across country at a faster rate than expected.

Specific sets of cards can be designed to cover the eventualities peculiar to a battle. They may, for instance, control the death of the Imperialist cavalry commander Pappenheim at Lützen, which affected his cavalry so much that their promising counterattack faded away, taking with it the Imperialists' last chance of saving the battle. Here is a set of Chance Cards to cover the numerous possibilities in this situation, bearing in mind that what occurred in fact must seem the most likely eventuality.

Card No 1 Only the front rank sees Pappenheim fall, but it is forced onwards by the press of horsemen behind.

Card No. 2 Both front and second ranks see their leader fall and involuntarily ease up, so dissipating the impetus of their charge.

Card No. 3 Seeing Pappenheim fall, his cavalry force reins up and halts for a game-move.

---

[7] See *Donald Featherstone's Battle Notes for Wargamers, Solo Wargaming Edition (2010)*

Card No. 4 Seeing Pappenheirn fall, his cavalry force reins up and halts for two game-moves.

Card No. 5 Seeing Pappenheim fall, his cavalry force reins up but, within half a move, is urged on by the entreaties of the second-in-command, now its leader.

Card No. 6 Realising that its leader has been killed, Pappenheim's cavalry force slows to a trot, thus losing the bonus effects of their charge.

Card No. 7 Realising that their beloved Pappenheim has been killed, the cavalry force carries on but with a reduced morale status.

As in every battle of military history, each engagement described here presents situations with opportunities for adding interest, and often realism, by the use of Chance Cards. The imaginative wargamer, indeed, may need to show restraint in their use at times.

**Military Possibilities**
Under analysis, every battle reveals stages when certain moves or tactics point the path to eventual victory or defeat. At each stage there are possible alternative courses of action to that taken, and some of these logical Military Possibilities may well lead to a complete reversal of the result. In some cases the course of action indicated by a Military Possibility results in a more reasonable and credible result than occurred on the historic field, but they must never be considered as excuses for indulging in whims and fancies, merely to 'see what happens'. Like real war, wargames are competitive contests influenced by luck, which is represented on table-top terrains by the throw of a die or the turn of a Chance Card — simple methods of simulating the ebb-and-flow and the fluctuations of war.

Military Possibilities can be utilised as a means of encouraging the wargamer representing the defeated commander cheerfully to accept his sub-standard role by giving him an outside chance of reversing the result, without radically altering the historical course of the battle. They should be restricted, therefore, to relatively minor aspects that may bring about increasingly interesting tactical twists. Abounding in all battles, Military Possibilities bring colour to the wargames table in proportion to the ingenuity of the wargamer.

Every battle described herein presents its own peculiar Military Possibility. Had the Imperialist commander at Pavia in 1525 not restrained his troops from plundering the French base camp, his foremost units of Italian and Spanish arquebusiers might not have reached the hedges and the copses, where they played a decisive part in throwing back the Swiss mercenaries and French cavalry. During the defence of the defile of Arques, an outflanking force of Catholic cavalry found itself unable to negotiate the marsh, but had it been a trifle less deep or the horses stronger, this force appearing on Henry's flank would undoubtedly have brought him to defeat.

## Conclusion

So many tactical features of the period appear in these battles that wargamers transforming themselves into the respective commanders will savour excitement and triumph, and suffer disappointment and defeat. The circumstances and course of each of these engagements may also be transferred to another period of military history and be fought with quite different troops: for example, the Imperialist Army at Pavia can be turned into Wellington's army defeating a French force in the Peninsula nearly three hundred years later; and the redoubtable Swedes of Gustavus Adolphus at Breitenfeld or Lutzen can be converted into equally redoubtable Prussians under Frederick the Great, and fight the Austrians one hundred years later.

# 1. The Battle of Ravenna 11 April 1512

THIS BATTLE was the first example of an action won by complete dominance in artillery - in this case under the control of an intelligent commander, and of Ferrara, one of the foremost artillerymen of his time. To relieve Ravenna, besieged by a French army commanded by Gaston de Foix, Duke of Nemours, the Spanish-Papal force, led by Ramon de Cardona, had taken up a position some two miles from the city in a flat waterlogged area backed by the River Ronco and flanked by marshy ground. Except for a twenty yard gap left between its northern end and the high bank of the Ronco, and a similar gap left at the southern end to allow cavalry to charge out in close column, the Spanish line was solid. They planted their 30 guns along the centre of the entrenchment. It is recorded that they also had some two-wheeled 'carts', each with a long frontally projecting spear and flanking scythe-blades, mounted with a bunch of arquebuses which, by mechanical means, could be fired as one. It seems that the carts were to be pushed forward by a long pole so as to break up the formation of an attacking column or to blunt a cavalry attack. There is no record, however, of their use at Ravenna.

Gaston de Foix marched out at the head of 23.000 men, leaving 2,000 Italian foot to guard his camp and trenches and hold off sorties from the beleaguered city. He formed up his army facing and conforming to the Spanish position, largely with the infantry drawn back in the centre and the cavalry thrown forward on the wings. La Palice, with 900 lances, was placed on the river flank with 30 guns and 3,500 Gascon foot, mostly crossbowmen. On their left were 500 German landsknechts under Jacob Empser, next to 3,000 Picard and Gascon infantry under the Seneschal of Normandy. To the left again were 780 French lances, flanked by 2,000 Italian infantry. The right wing was completed by 24 guns under the Duke of Ferrara, a famed artillery expert of the day, flanked by 2,000 French light horse composed of mounted arquebusiers, cross-bowmen and stradiots (light cavalrymen).

The Spaniards allowed the French army to advance within cannon shot of their entrenchments, although Colonna, the Spanish cavalry leader, was refused permission by Cardona to charge out and attack the vulnerable heads of the columns as they were crossing the river by the French Bridge. The advancing French halted and gazed at the Spanish position, but could see only masses of cavalry on the right and left and some ominously sited guns. The cavalry were Colonna's 670 Italian lances next to the river and Pescara's 1,700 light horse (Spanish ginetes and Italian mounted arquebusiers) on the Spanish right; there was a reserve of 565 lances on the river bank in the rear of the position. Four bodies of Spanish infantry, each 1,000 strong, were lying down behind the trench in the flattest part of the position,

# The Battle of RAVENNA
## 11th April 1512

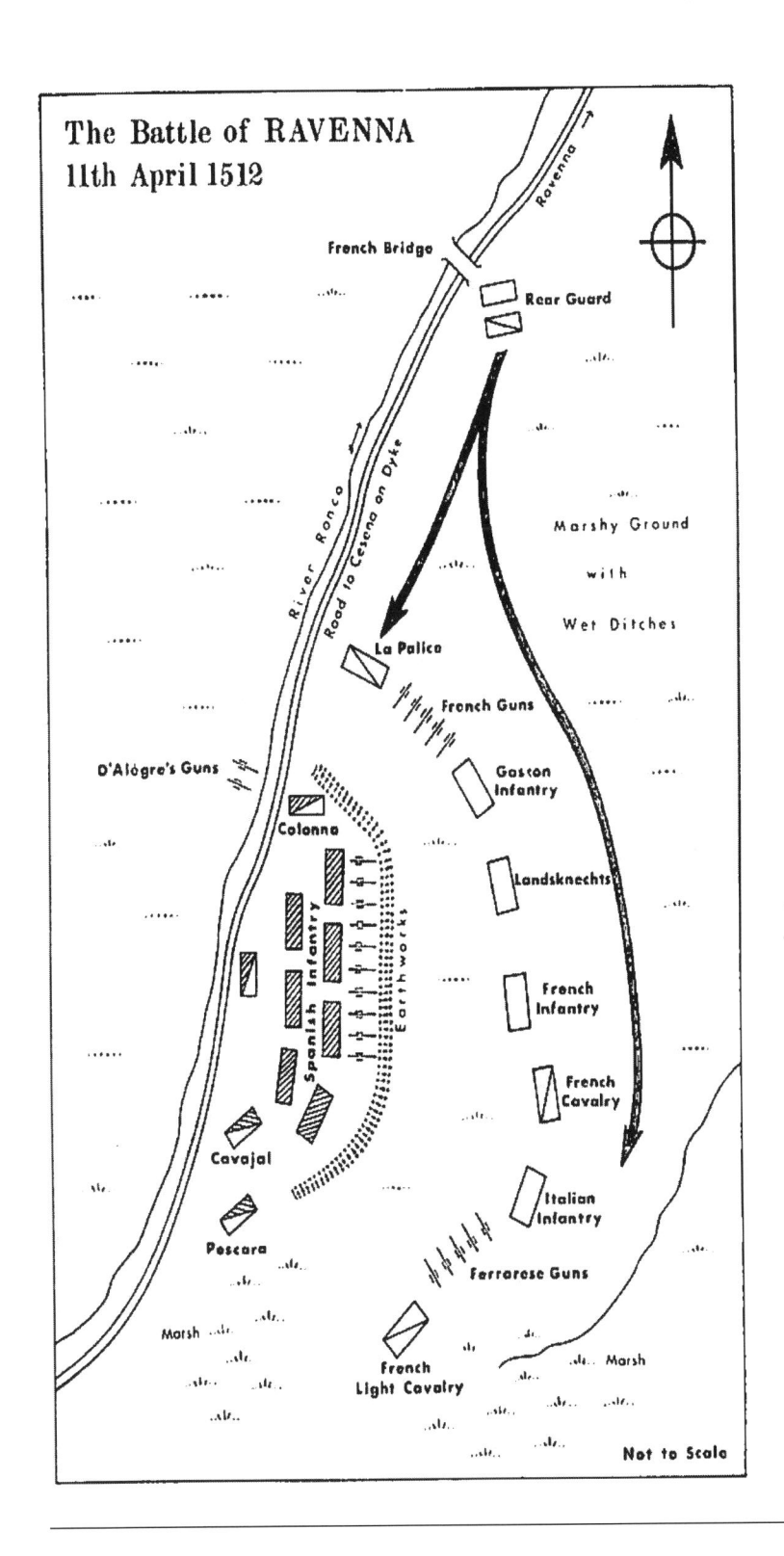

and three Spanish foot regiments and 2,000 Italian foot of the Papal levy remained in reserve, making a total infantry strength of about 11,000.

This was a period when armies attacked once they were in position, but at Ravenna Gaston adopted different tactics, holding his troops in check for two hours whilst his artillery pounded the Spanish lines. The guns in front of his right wing and near the river played upon the only target they could see - Colonna's cavalry - while Ferrara's guns enfiladed Carvajal's and Pescara's Light Horse. The Spanish guns in their turn so effectively hit the Gascons that they fell back against the flanks of the landsknechts. With neither army showing any inclination to come to grips, Gaston de Foix sent d'Alegre with two guns to a position on the far side of the river whence they could fire into the rear of Colonna's cavalry.

Realising that there was little point in allowing his cavalry to be decimated without striking a blow, the Spanish commander sent Carvajal's corps and Pescara's ginetes from his right wing out over the marshy ground in a series of charges on the French light horse and the Ferrarese guns they were guarding. After a surging cavalry mêlée into which Cardona fed his cavalry reserve, the French reinforced their horsemen and eventually drove the Spanish cavalry back. Simultaneously, on the other flank, Colonna's cavalry had charged La Palice's cavalry, but they were driven off in confusion - the survivors fleeing south-westwards down the road to the protection of the entrenched Spanish infantry. The victorious French cavalry pursued on both flanks.

While the cavalry battles raged on the wings, Gaston de Foix ordered his infantry, which had been taking heavy punishment from the Spanish artillery, to advance, and 2,000 Gascon crossbowmen supported by 1,000 Picardy pikemen went forward. As they neared the enemy position, the Spanish infantry rose and at close range poured such a blast of fire into them that the French foot soldiers melted away, their survivors fleeing back to safety.

In spite of the serious impediment of a drainage ditch across their line of advance, Empser's landsknechts, in a great column of pikemen, now assaulted the Spanish position. When they closed in combat, Spanish sword-and-buckler men from the rear ranks slipped in among them and inflicted heavy casualties. After a short, sharp struggle the landsknechts were thrown back, leaving many dead before the entrenchment. The Spaniards, sensing victory, raised a loud shout, but that was quite misplaced because the dispersal of their flanking cavalry had already lost them the battle.

In a second charge Gascon .and other French infantry and the German landsknechts traversed the ditch before being repelled with heavy losses, the Gascons being charged in flank by the remnants of Colonna's cavalry. At the same moment two companies of Spanish infantry charged forward from their position and broke into the shattered Gascon ranks, fighting their way through until they found themselves isolated in the rear of the French line.

The infantry battle seemed to have reached deadlock, but the position was dramatically changed as masses of French cavalry, mainly from La Palice's division, began to penetrate the gap at the river end of the Spanish position. Charged by cavalry in flank and rear and attacked again in front by rallied French foot, the Spanish infantry battalions broke. All were ridden down except a solid body of about 2,000 who escaped in close formation south-eastwards down the Cesena road. Attempting to escape also, along a narrow raised path by the river, the broken column of the two isolated Spanish companies previously mentioned was pointed out to Gaston de Foix, the French commander. At once, with his personal staff of some 15-20 gentlemen, he charged up on to the raised path to intercept them, only to be met by a volley of arquebus fire, followed by a charge with levelled pikes that brought down and captured every French horseman, including the army commander!

So ended one of the bloodiest battles of the age, with both armies suffering huge losses. The vanquished Spaniards were almost exterminated, only some 300 cavalry and about 3,000 infantry remaining out of the 16,000 who had stood seemingly secure behind entrenchments at dawn.

Gaston de Foix, the French commander, used his superior artillery strength skilfully against entrenched infantry and artillery. Had he halted his infantry outside the range of the Spanish artillery, his losses would have been far less. The Spanish defensive tactics required a superiority of artillery fire they did not possess, for to win this battle the Spanish had to silence the French artillery with fewer guns —an impossible task. With every part of the position within reach of cannon shot, the Spanish cavalry were sitting ducks, and the rest of the army, in a murderous cul-de-sac with a river at their backs, had as their only line of retreat one extreme end of their position that was under artillery fire.

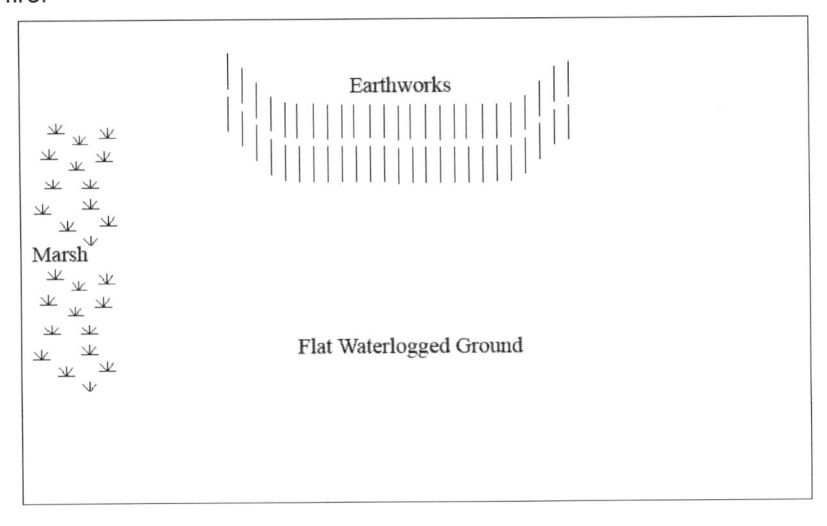

### Reconstructing the Battle as a Wargame
This can be a good straightforward wargame, although the 'Spanish' commander's course of action will be dictated by the 'French' commander; if he uses artillery as did de Foix, the Spanish cavalry will be forced out of their entrenchments as in real life, and the game will closely resemble its real-life counterpart. Considered as a wargame, the battle is a test of the fighting qualities of each side, with the Spanish at a slight disadvantage because of the French guns and their own badly sited position.

The river behind the Spaniards need not be reproduced on the tabletop terrain, but its known presence dictates that they stay and fight it out. This means that d'Alegre's guns will be 'off-the-table', having arrived at a predetermined point (unknown to the Spaniards until they open fire). Their movement can be controlled by Chance Cards. In 1512 there was no way in which the Spaniards could reply to their fire, so the same situation should apply on the wargames table.

Set up the game with the Spaniards in their historical dispositions and the French out of cannon range, as in 1512.

Endeavour to select a French commander without knowledge of the battle.

### Classification of Commanders
The French commander, Gaston de Foix, must be graded as 'above average', and Cardona, the Spanish commander, just 'average', because of the faulty siting of his position. Had de Foix fought the battle in the generally accepted manner of the day, however, Cardona's defensive tactics would probably have proved victorious.

### Quality of Troops and Morale
The troops on both sides were good average soldiers, none showing up badly. There is no need to under-classify any of them to ensure a good and authentic wargame. The artillery on the French side undoubtedly won the battle. The morale of all formations was first-class, fluctuating according to circumstances as the battle progressed.

### Effect and Construction of Terrain
Although the battle was fought over an area of flat waterlogged ground without trees or shrubs, the terrain was all important, as the Spanish siting of their position lost them the battle. Its construction is simple, being the flat table surface with a simulated marsh on one wing. The Spanish earthworks can be constructed of polystyrene, suitably cut and earth coloured, or plasticine.

### Military Possibilities
Once Cardona had made up his mind to stay strictly on the defensive, there were few Military Possibilities. If he is made to take any other course of action, it is no longer the Battle of Ravenna. Had de Foix fought in the old accepted manner by attacking without the preliminary

bombardment, his tactics would have failed disastrously and the result would most likely have been reversed.

## 2. The Battle of Pavia 24 February 1525

THIS DECISIVE battle of the Italian Wars of the first half of the sixteenth century was a 'victory by surprise', when an incautious enemy was caught before he could get into battle array. From 28 October 1524 throughout the worst months of winter, Pavia and its garrison of Spanish troops and landsknecht mercenaries were besieged by a French army led by King Francis I.

After three months of gross discomfort, made worse by lack of pay, the troops of both armies had become discontented to the point of mutiny. Then, in late January, came a relieving Imperialist army under the joint command of Lannoy (the Spanish Viceroy of Naples) and the Marquis of Pescara, but, with only 1,000 cavalry and some 17,000 infantry, they were much inferior to the French in numbers. So, rather than engage against the odds in a pitched battle, they endeavoured to force Francis to abandon the siege by threatening his communications with Milan and France — by throwing up defences on the eastern bank of the Vernacula brook, a deep-sunk and very muddy tributary of the River Ticino that in winter formed an almost impregnable barrier. To counter this, the French dug two miles of earthworks from the Ticino in the south, with their northern end resting on the wall of the Park of Mirabello, a hunting palace three miles north of Pavia; the south park wall was demolished to facilitate troop movements.

Then, as Italian and Swiss mercenaries blockaded the western aspect of Pavia, the two armies exchanged intermittent fire across the brook, in some places separated by only forty yards of mud and water, both praying that the hard weather, general discomfort and lack of pay would cause the enemy's unreliable mercenaries to desert and go home. In mid-February that was what happened, for both of Francis's mercenary Italian companies disbanded when their leader died through wounds, and only two days later 6,000 Grison Swiss mercenaries marched off to clear their borders from an invading Milanese army. Thus, in a three-day period, the French lost 8,000 men.

Francis was now in the unenviable position of attempting to besiege Pavia while holding off the relieving force with an army reduced to 1,300 mounted men-at-arms, 12,500 landsknechts, 5,000 Swiss of various cantons and about 9,000 French and Italian infantry. Even so, his force possessed numerical parity with Lannoy's and was stronger in cavalry.

The Imperialists were also having trouble with their own Swiss mercenaries, who were demanding overdue pay or immediate battle, which fact, coupled with the encouraging news from the enemy camp, decided them to take the offensive. On the night of 23-4 February, with their artillery vigorously bombarding the entrenchments on the far side of the Vernacula, the Imperialist army marched two miles upstream in what the terminology of the time called a *camisade* - because they wore shirts over their armour for recognition on the dark, wet and windy night. There were five divisions of infantry in this attempt to turn the French flank: the first division comprised Italian and Spanish arquebusiers with 200 light horse, preceded by 2.000 pioneers carrying battering rams and tools; the second consisted of Spanish infantry under Pescara, followed by half the cavalry; the third Lannoy and the German landsknechts, followed by the other half of the cavalry; the fourth a corps of German mercenaries under the renegade Constable Bourbon, and the last a rear column of Spanish and Italian foot.

Reaching the north-east corner of the park walls without interruption, they breached them and passed through into the park to form up in an area of partly opened rides and lawns, suitable for limited manoeuvres. With considerable difficulty the foremost units were restrained from dispersing to plunder the French base camp, where the light cavalry were left. Francis, finding his flank turned and the enemy forming up steadily behind his headquarters, left the greater part of the French infantry holding the southern section of the Vernacula and, in the early light of dawn, formed up the main body of his gendarmerie, with the landsknechts on their right and the Swiss on the left. He could not use the Italian infantry watching the west walls of Pavia because they were occupied by the distraction of a pre-arranged sally from the city. The Duc d'Alencon with 300 lances and some companies of Italian and French foot remained in camp to the north-east of Pavia and never came into action at all. Advancing with his cavalry and a few guns, Francis opened fire upon the last enemy column (the Spanish-Italian division) as it was passing through the broken walls, then charged with two squadrons of gendarmerie, to send them fleeing back as far as the Vernacula and abandoning several pieces of artillery on the way. The rest of the French cavalry coming up, Francis placed himself at their head and charged across the front of his own guns (so masking their fire) into the hindmost of the two Imperialist cavalry brigades in the centre of the enemy line. Their leader killed, the Burgundian and Austrian horsemen of this brigade scattered, leaving a gap in the left centre of the Imperialist army into which Francis led his horsemen in repeated charges on the neighbouring infantry columns, putting them into disorder but failing to break them. The French numbers rapidly diminished, however, as man after man was brought down by the fire of arquebusiers sheltering in hedges and copses out of reach of their lances, and they were falling into disarray.

At that point the Swiss and landsknecht mercenaries approached, but the former, moving slowly while being harassed by volleys from Del Vasto's arquebusiers on the Imperial right wing, only succeeded in putting in a desultory 'push of pike' before retreating en masse along the Milan road. Knowing their impetuous ferocity in the past, both friends and foes were astonished by their lack of dash. The fact was that the outmoded

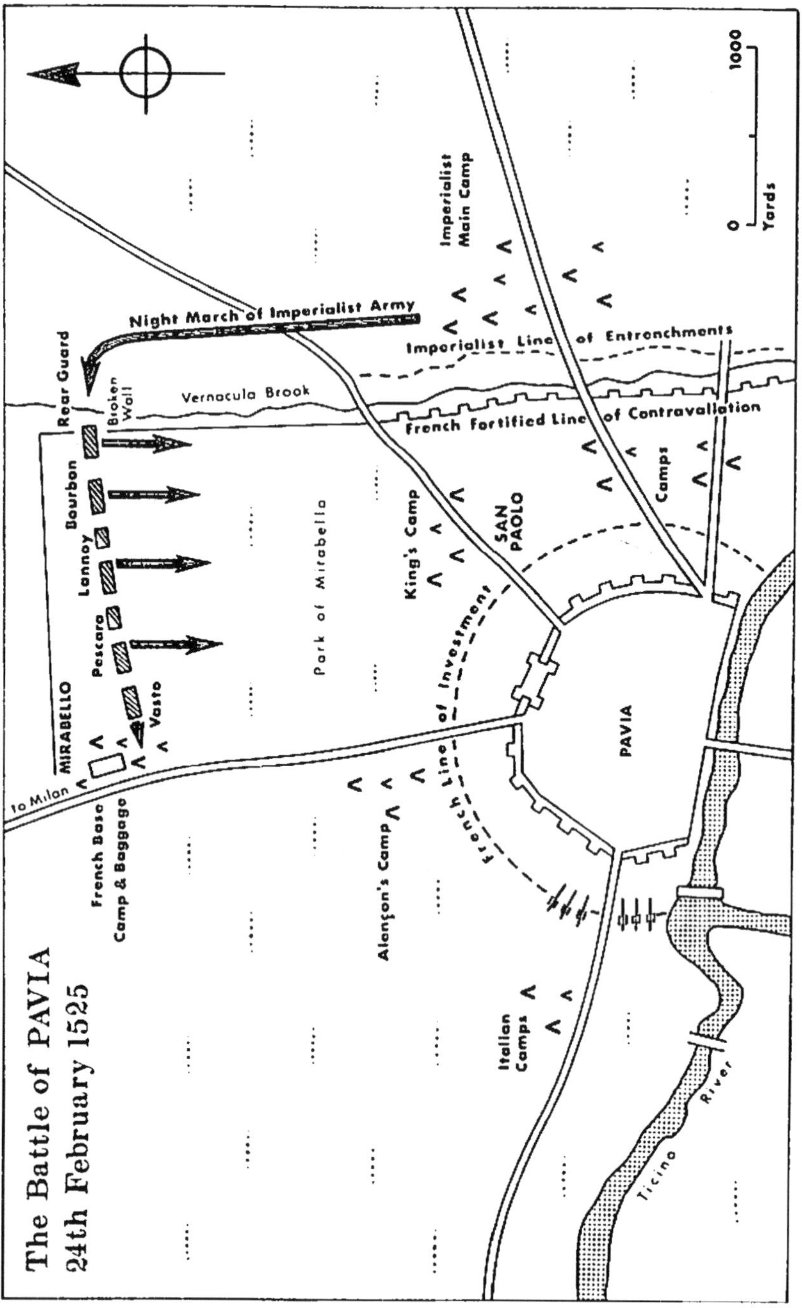

The Battle of PAVIA
24th February 1525
Night March of Imperialist Army
Imperialist Main Camp
Imperialist Line of Entrenchments
0
1000
Yards
Rear Guard
Broken Wall
Vernacula Brook
French Fortified Line of Contravallation
Bourbon
Lannoy
Pescara
Vasto
MIRABELLO
To Milan
French Base Camp & Baggage
Park of Mirabella
King's Camp
SAN PAOLO
Camps
French Line of Investment
PAVIA
Alençon's Camp
Italian Camps
Ticino River

tactics of the Swiss three years earlier in 1522 at Bicocca had cost them so dearly that they had lost their aggressiveness.

On the French right the landsknecht Black Bands launched themselves headlong into a column of their countrymen, commanded by Lannoy. The fighting was desperate until they were taken in flank by the other body of Imperialist landsknechts and wiped out almost to the last man. Finally the French infantry came up from the lines of contravallation, to be immediately attacked and routed by the same columns of landsknechts who had exterminated the Black Bands. The King and the remnants of his cavalry fought on until Francis was brought to the ground and captured.

Seeing that the day was lost, Alencon, who had remained passively out on the left throughout, taking no part except for a little feeble skirmishing with the Imperialist light horse, now marched from the field, taking with him the Italian troops who had been holding the western front of the lines of investment.

The French lost 8,000 men at Pavia, the slaughter among their nobility resembling that at Agincourt one hundred and ten years earlier. The Imperialists had 700 casualties, mostly from the cavalry corps ridden down by Francis early in the action.

Tactically, Pavia was an interesting battle, as both armies were on the move and came together in an irregular manner, with each division as it reached the front finding itself engaged by hostile troops. The battle emphasised the growing importance of small arms, as the arquebus fire was decisive in delaying the advance of the Swiss infantry, caused heavy casualties on the flanks of the French landsknecht column, and, perhaps most important of all, disorganised the French gendarmerie. Possessing few arquebusiers, their infantry being mainly armed with ineffective crossbows, the French were unable to send a force of light infantry against the Imperialist arquebusiers. Pavia encouraged the captains of the period to mass their arquebusiers, and led to a mistaken neglect of the pike, an essential weapon to repel cavalry.

**Reconstructing the Battle as a Wargame**

The crux of this simulation lies in the realistic timing of the Imperialist formations assembling in the Park as dawn approaches, King Francis striking in the half-light with a force of cavalry and artillery, and the remainder of his troops coming up at intervals. The wargame should start with the Imperialist troops set up as on the map, the Spanish/Italian infantry (their hindmost formation) just passing through the breach in the park wall. At this moment they are assailed by French artillery and then charged by Francis and his gendarmerie, who next turn and disperse an Imperialist cavalry force. No self-respecting wargamer is going to stand back and allow a surprise attack to be perpetrated by clearly visible troops, so the Imperialist commander must not be aware of this impending attack. To simulate its sudden emergence from the mist and half-light of early dawn, the gendarmerie

## Wargame Terrain for PAVIA (at start of battle)

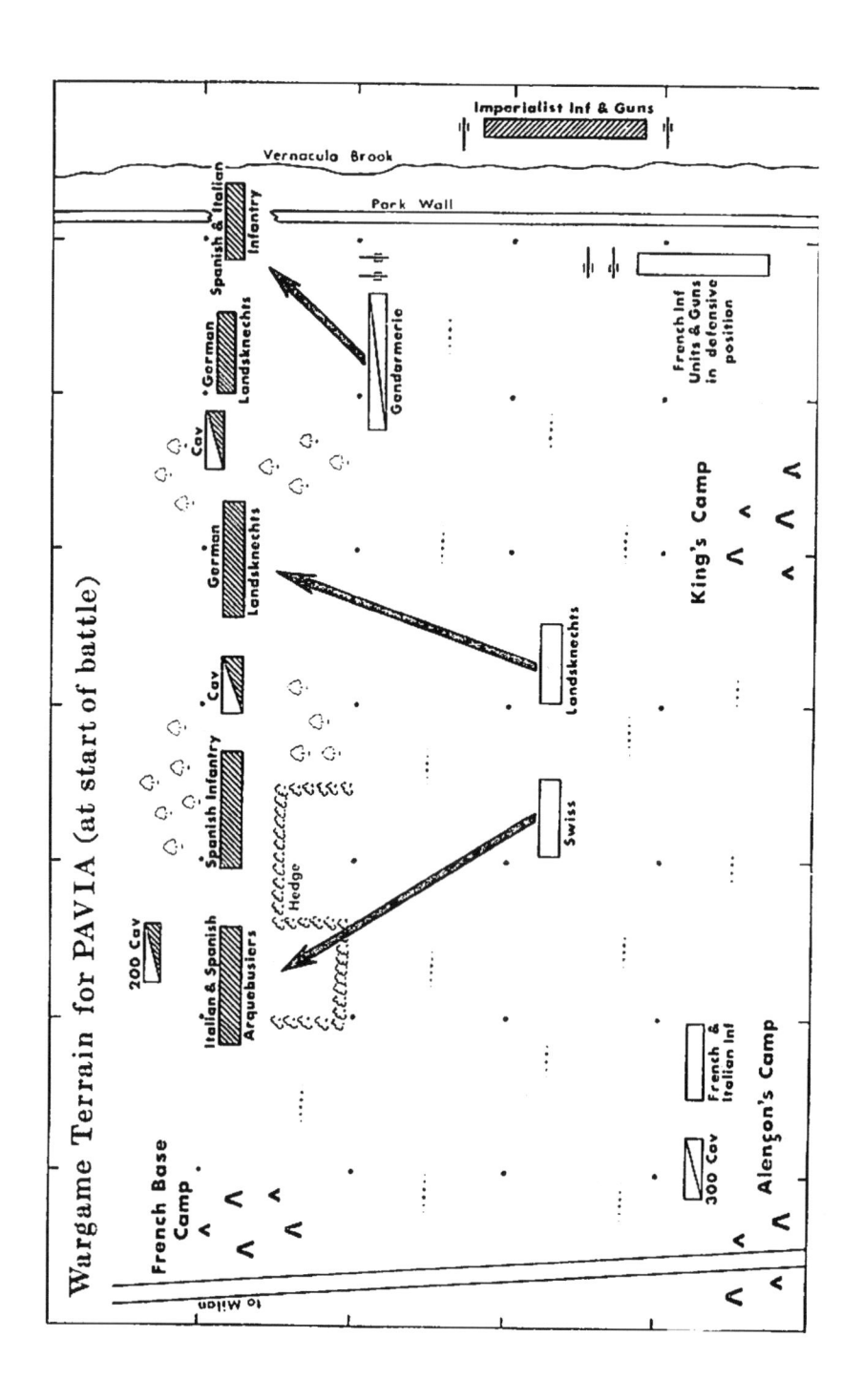

Imperialist Inf & Guns

Vernacula Brook

Park Wall

Spanish & Italian Infantry

*German Landsknechts

Cav

Gendarmerie

German Landsknechts

French Inf Units & Guns in defensive position

King's Camp

Spanish Infantry

*Cav

Landsknechts

Hedge

Swiss

Italian & Spanish Arquebusiers

200 Cav

French Base Camp

French & Italian Inf

300 Cav

Alençon's Camp

to Milan

and artillery are initially placed on the table within charge-move distance of their targets. The Swiss infantry and the landsknechts in the French service will be placed as indicated on the map, commencing their move forward from the start of the game.

The French commander will find it extremely frustrating to have Alencon with his force actually on the table but not coming to aid their hard-pressed comrades but, if historical authenticity is to be maintained, then this must be the case.

### Classification of Commanders
The Imperialist commanders, Lannoy and Pescara, must be graded 'above average', and King Francis, under the prevailing circumstances, 'average'.

### Quality of Troops and Morale
The Imperialist arquebusiers were excellent and probably turned the battle. The French gendarmerie were first-class troops and did all that could be expected of them. The Swiss in the French pay, in their military twilight, were undoubtedly poor; otherwise the mercenaries on both sides fought extremely well, even against their own countrymen.

The morale of all troops was first-class, with the exception of the Swiss, whose morale must be graded second-class, and fluctuated with the course of the battle. On the day the behaviour of the mercenaries renders it unnecessary to evoke any of the usual 'mercenary' rulings.

### Effect and Construction of Terrain
The hedges and copses in the park enabled the arquebusiers to be highly effective. Use the flat table surface, with the brook running down on one wing, paralleled by the park wall. Make the copses very open, as much action occurs within them.

### Military Possibilities
Had Alencon's force intervened, it might have made a difference, but such an intervention detracts from historical authenticity and should be resisted, unless it promises to improve the wargame. Similarly, authenticity suffers if the march of the Imperialist flanking force is discovered earlier, so allowing Francis to mass his troops instead of bringing them on to the field piecemeal.

Perhaps the most important Military Possibility arises from the Imperialist commander managing to restrain his troops from over-much plundering of the French base camp on the eastern aspect of the Park. If the foremost units, the Italian and Spanish arquebusiers, had dispersed in search of loot, they may well have been followed by the Spanish infantry behind them — a course of action that would have deprived the Imperialists of the valuable services of the arquebusiers stationed behind the hedges and in the copses to throw back the Swiss mercenaries and the French cavalry.

Presumably Lannoy and his Imperialists had some artillery, but it is not known how much or how it was used.

# 3. The Battle of Mohacs 29 August 1526

ALTHOUGH THE opposing Turkish army, before whom the Hungarians had been slowly withdrawing, was numerically superior, the military pride of the Europeans caused them to stand and accept battle on the plain of Mohacs. Their army was made up of some 12,000 horse — 8,000 lightly equipped 'hussars' and 4,000 fully armoured nobles and their retinues — and 13,000 foot, of whom 5,500 were veteran foreign mercenaries and the rest local levies experienced in border warfare in their mountain regions. The young King Louis of Hungary commanded the army, with Archbishop Tomori and George Zapolya as Generals-in-Chief, besides numerous soldier-bishops and a veteran Polish condottiere, Leonard Gnomski.

The Turks had in the field an army of 60-70,000 men, formed of 35,000 feudal horse (Roumeliot, Bosnian and Anatolian), 15,000 Janissaries and regular horse, and a horde of ill-armed irregular horse and foot (Azabs). Their very considerable artillery force was partly manned by Italian and German renegade gunners.

The Hungarians drew up for battle inland from the town of Mohacs, mile from the marshy bank of the Danube, overflowing through recent rains. The ground, flat and featureless and ideal for cavalry operations, sloped gently up towards the hills concealing the Turks. To avoid being outflanked the Hungarians formed up in two long lines, the front line composed of 10,000 infantry in dense columns interspersed with 6,000 cavalry, including much of the feudal horse of the barons. Their 20 guns were placed in the centre. The right was held by the Croatian levies under Francis Bathiani, and the left was commanded by Peter Perenni, the Ban of Temesvar, who was greatly experienced in frontier fights against the Turks. The second line, in two ranks, was formed of 3,000 foot and 6,000 horse, with three squadrons of feudal horse in front of the King and his selected guard of 1,000 fully armoured knights, who were flanked by the Bishop's levies. Two small bodies of infantry were posted as flank guards, and there may have been a few light cavalry scouts beyond them.

The Turkish leader, the Sultan Soliman, who had captured Rhodes in the previous year, formed his army in unusually deep order to counter the tempestuous fury of the charges of the heavy armoured knights, so that the Roumeliot horse occupied the first of three ranks, the Anatolian horse the second, and the Janissaries, flanked by Spahis and Silladar squadrons, the third. There were 80 guns, chained together in a huge battery between the second and third ranks. Parties of irregular cavalry called Akindjis were scattered in front of the army, and about a mile forward, out on the left front, more of them, plus 4,000 Bosnian horse, were placed behind hills to form an outflanking force when battle was joined.

Concealed behind the hills, the main Turkish army was slow getting into battle order, and it was not until three hours after noon that the lance-heads and pennons of the Turkish horse appeared on the hill-tops. The Hungarians, who had been drawn up since early morning, opened fire as soon as the Roumeliot horsemen came within range, but with little effect, and then, as the Turkish horse seemed about to charge, the whole Hungarian front line surged forward to push everything before it, thrusting the Roumeliot horse back on the Anatolian cavalry of the second line in a mêlée in which the lighter Turkish cavalry suffered heavy casualties. It is likely that this relatively light resistance by the Turkish horse was a tactical move to disorder the Hungarians, whose infantry could not keep up with their charging horsemen, and draw them on to the massed Turkish guns.

Messengers from the fighting came back to the King with news that the whole Turkish army was giving way and now was the time for the Hungarian 'Main-Battle' to advance and clinch the victory. So, passing through their own guns, the second Hungarian line rolled forward up the slope to reinforce the tumultuous mêlée. Fighting fiercely, the Hungarians forced their way through the wilting ranks of both Anatolian and Roumeliot horse until they reached the Janissaries of the third line and the chained guns. Here they were brought to a halt, milling about on open ground, charging and countercharging as salvoes of roundshot at ranges of less than a hundred yards caused them heavy casualties.

As the Croatian infantry on the Hungarian right had struggled forward, trying to maintain contact with their cavalry, the Turkish outflanking cavalry force had come thundering into them, to send them reeling back and forcing the cavalry of the second Hungarian line to throw back their right squadrons to form a new front. Then, in the 'killing-ground' before the Turkish guns, the sadly stricken Hungarians began to wilt and the disordered cavalry and infantry of their left wing gave way, to retire to marshy ground near the Danube, where they tried to rally. But then the centre, unable to endure the point-blank discharges any longer and much affected by the suffocating smoke, gave way in great disorder. They passed through their own guns and skirted the camp on the outskirts of Mohacs, which was already being attacked by Turkish light horsemen. Completely beaten, the Hungarians made no attempt to rally. The Turks were prevented from carrying out a general pursuit by trumpets ordering every man to muster by a standard and remain in his original position.

About half the Hungarian army perished—only 3,000 out of the 13,000 foot got away, with 7,000 or 8,000 cavalry. The heavily armoured knights, having charged so fiercely that their armoured horses were too exhausted to carry them out of the battle when the rout began, fared far worse than the light hussars. Every Hungarian leader was left on the field, and all the noble houses of Hungary suffered loss: only five of the numerous prisoners were spared, the remainder being decapitated on the spot. The body of King Louis was

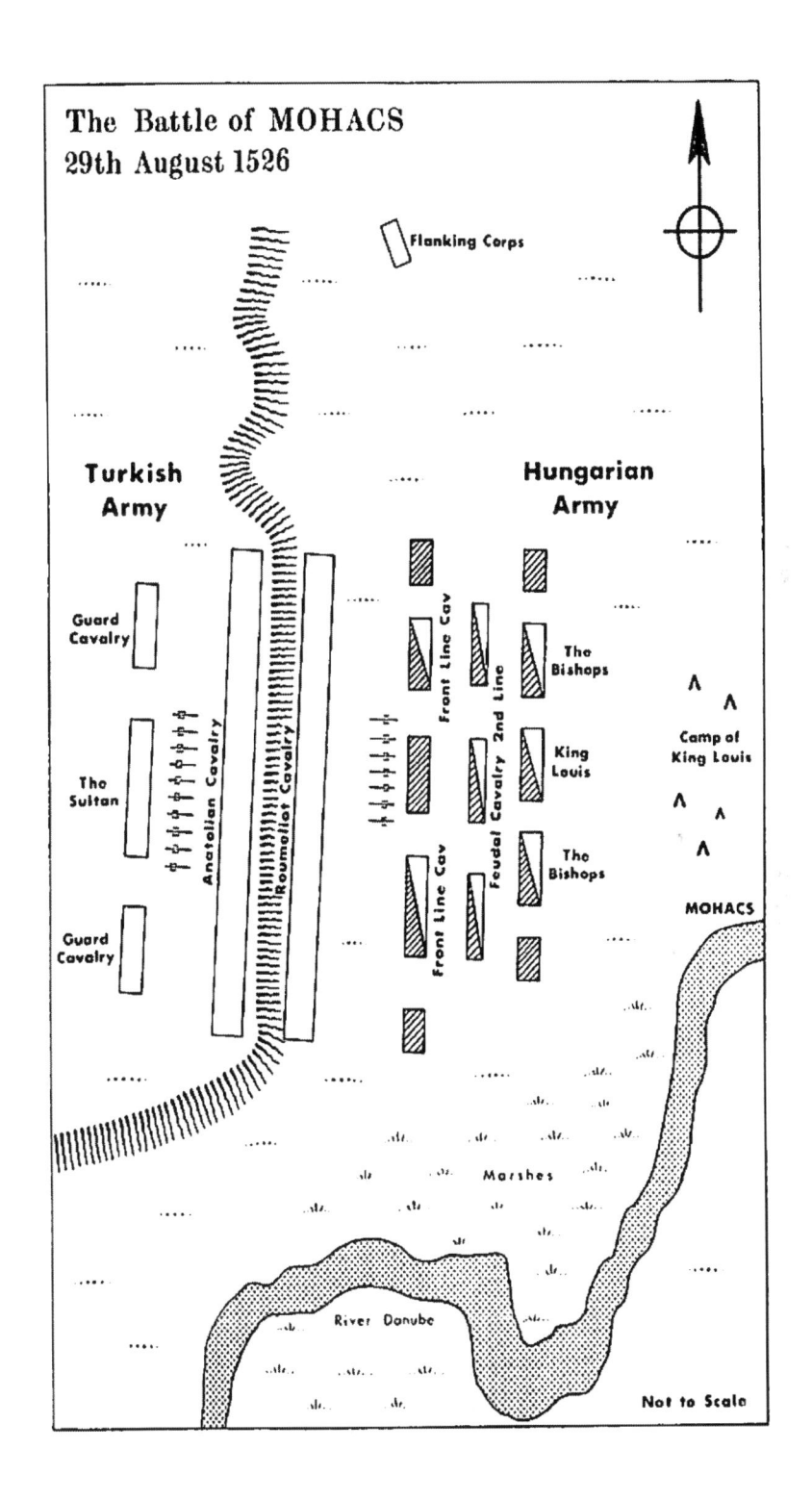

# The Battle of MOHACS
## 29th August 1526

found two months later, the subsiding Danube floods revealing the heavily armoured rider and horse at the bottom of a gully a mile from the battlefield. Turkish losses, although heavy, were much less than those of the defeated Hungarians.

## Reconstructing the Battle as a Wargame

Ideally the 'Hungarian' commander should go into the battle without knowing the numerical odds against him. Set out the Hungarian force in its historical formation, with its front rank about 18 inches from the baseline (about two game-moves' distance). The Turkish commander should send his front rank of Roumeliot horse on to the table at the first game-move, to advance steadily until within range of the Hungarian guns. On the second game-move, he will send on the line of Anatolian horse, which will advance in the wake of the Roumeliots. When the latter come into artillery range, they will take fire for one move, and then the Hungarian front rank will charge. Being heavier, elite cavalry, they will almost certainly push back the Turkish light cavalrymen, who have already suffered casualties from artillery fire. Thus the Hungarian front rank will advance across the table, pushing before them the retreating Turkish light horse until the latter reach a point within about 18 inches (two game-moves) of their own baseline.

While the Turkish light cavalry is retreating in disorder, the Turkish guns, the third line of Janissaries and their elite cavalry are placed on the table. The Hungarian commander, flushed with the success of his front line, will very likely have already pushed forward the remainder of his troops to support them, thinking, just as did King Louis, that he will make victory certain. But, in any event, it should be mandatory for him to do so on the move *previous* to that on which the Turkish third line is placed on its baseline. Having reconstructed the authentic situation of the disordered Hungarian force coming up against a massed battery of guns, backed by the cream of the Turkish army, the wargame will inevitably take the same course as it did in 1526.

The existence of the outflanking Turkish cavalry force was known to the Hungarians, but their small scouting party reported that the Turks did not seem inclined to attack, so the Hungarians declined to break the formation of their ranks. To simulate this situation, the Hungarian commander should be told (without undue emphasis) that there is a relatively small cavalry force on his right flank. He is then free to take whatever steps he desires.

## Classification of Commanders

Soliman was undoubtedly a good tactician and, not relying blindly on his numerical superiority, as many commanders of his day would have done, he employed intelligent tactics to draw his more heavily armed enemy on to the already prepared and highly suitable 'killing-ground' that lay before his massed batteries of guns. So he must be classified 'above average'. King Louis, the Hungarian leader, must be rated as 'average', if only to ensure that he orders forward his second rank when he is informed, optimistically, that he is winning the battle.

# Wargame Terrain for MOHACS (at end of 1st game-move)

Roumelior Light Horse

Gentle Slope

(20 Guns)

Hungarian Army

## Quality of Troops and Morale
The Hungarian mounted armoured knights, the Turkish Janissaries, the Spahis and Silladars are all elite troops and should be given the usual bonuses on dice throws etc, to represent their superior morale and ability. The remainder of the troops on both sides are 'average', with the exception of the irregulars and levies of both Hungarian and Turkish armies, who were 'below average'.

Initially the morale of all troops can be first-class, and it can fluctuate in the usual manner as the battle progresses.

## Effect and Construction of Terrain
The hills are important because they controlled the course of the battle, concealing the strength and dispositions of the Turkish force, and aiding their outflanking cavalry body. The terrain is easily constructed, the Hungarian half of the table being flat, and sloping gently up from the mid-point to the Turkish baseline along its entire length.

## Military Possibilities
The battle might have taken a different course if the Hungarian front line had not charged so precipitately, but had employed its artillery to greater effect before moving forward. Having dispersed the Roumeliot and Anatolian horse, the Hungarians had achieved relative parity with their Turkish opponents, and they might have awaited a Turkish attack with a better end result. However, this was really outside the scope of the feudal and chivalrous character of the Hungarian armoured knights. Precautions might have been taken against the outflanking Turkish cavalry force but, with the Hungarian right and centre collapsing soon after the Croatians had been outflanked, this course of action is really academic.

An interesting possibility seems to have occurred on the day of the battle but, if carried out on the wargames table, it would alter the course of the action radically. Seemingly, Gnomski, the Polish condottiere, advocated using the old Hussite tactics, i.e. covering the flanks and rear of the army with massed waggons, in the hope that the Turks would attack frontally in the face of artillery and missile-carrying infantry. Assuming that the Turks were beaten off, the whole Hungarian army could then sally out in a counterattack, to achieve a complete victory. The success of this plan would have been doubtful, however, against a wily Turkish commander who had shown himself disinclined to commit his army to a serious frontal attack. Faced with a Hungarian army protected in this way, lie was far more likely to manoeuvre round the flanks and cut the enemy off from their camps and stores in and around Mohacs. Then, surrounded by greatly superior numbers, they would be forced to break out of their fortified camp or be starved into submission.

## 4. The Battle of Ceresole 14 April 1544

THE BATTLE of Ceresole was unique in that both sides drew up their forces in careful array with the fixed intention of fighting, although each commander was aware that hazarding all on a general action was a dangerous business. It was an engagement emphasising that the infantry of the day—arquebusiers, Swiss and landsknecht pikemen — when fighting with other infantry, were helpless if attacked by cavalry, and that the latter, by repeated charges, could pin steady infantry without necessarily breaking them.

During the winter of 1543-4 the young Enghien was besieging Carignano, a strongly held Spanish fortress sited in the middle of an area of French positions, in an attempt to force the Spanish Marquis del Vasto to try and relieve it. His action stimulated 100 gallant young noblemen of the French Court to post full speed to the area in the hope of winning glory and fame. Closely watched by French light cavalry, del Vasto came into the area with a force of 7,000 landsknechts, 6,000 Italian foot, some 5,000 Spanish and German infantry who were veterans of African campaigns, 300 Florentine and 300 Neapolitan light horse and 200 Spanish and Italian heavy-armed gendarmerie, and 20 guns. Del Vasto believed the steadiness of his German infantry, plus large numbers of arquebusiers, would balance his shortage of cavalry.

Determined to fight on his own chosen ground, Enghien selected a position on a long low hillside with gentle slopes, facing a similar ridge. The flanks could only be seen from the centre sections of the ridges as both centres stood higher than their wings. A farm and outbuilding lay before the centre of the Spanish line and another in front of their right wing, and there was a small wood on the French right. The French army was divided in the old style into three corps — the 'Battle' (centre) under Enghien, the 'Vaward' (right) under de Boutieres and the 'Rearward' (left) under Dampierre. There was no second line or reserve. The line running from right to left comprised 3 companies of light cavalry (450/500 men), 400 French infantry, de Boulieres with 80 men-at-arms of the gendarmerie, a pike column of 13 veteran Swiss companies, Enghien himself at the head of 3 companies (250) of gendarmerie, 150 light horse and the 100 gentlemen volunteers from Paris, 3,000 so-called Swiss pikemen provided by the Count of Gruyeres, 6 companies of Italian infantry, and, on the extreme left, 400 mounted archers acting as light cavalry.

Both armies were endeavouring to keep under cover —the French/Swiss mercenaries were lying-down behind the crest of the hill — and neither side was fully visible as the Imperialists began to deploy on the forward slope. In an effort to discover the French dispositions, and perhaps turn their flanks, del Vasto sent out a screen of 800 arquebusiers to skirmish with their counterparts from the French and Italian companies in a scattering of fire-fights that flickered up and down the slopes between the lines for nearly four hours. It is said to have been 'a pretty sight ... for they played off on each other all the ruses and stratagems of petty war'. Meanwhile both sides brought up their artillery, the Spanish placing their 20 guns beside the two farms, and Enghien deploying two batteries each of 10 guns, one in front of the Gruyeres contingent on his left and the other in front of the Swiss in the centre. While the skirmishers bickered, the guns fired incessantly in a largely ineffective manner, as both sides were still under cover. Del Vasto sent the Florentine horse to take the arquebusiers in flank, but Enghien replied by pushing des Thermes' light horse fonvard on his right wing and easily scattered them.

Now del Vasto took the general offensive by advancing across the dip between the two armies, revealing on his left wing the Italian foot under the Prince of Salerno flanked by the 300 Florentine horse, 7,000 landsknechts in the centre, 200 lance-armed gendarmerie on their right under his own command, and Cardona with 5,000 Spanish and German veterans, flanked by Lannoy with 300 Neapolitan horse, on the right wing. The shaken Florentine horse were pushed back on to the pikes of Salerno's infantry, who were simultaneously assailed by des Thermes' horsemen following up. Although disordered, the Italians held their ground, but in the time required by Salerno to get them under control, the Spanish centre had run into real trouble.

Here the 7,000 Landsknechts had advanced well up the slope while the Gascon infantry of the French right centre had moved downhill to attack Salerno's Italians. Seeing their exposed flanks, the Gascons swerved diagonally left towards the German column. Excellently controlled, the great mass of landsknechts split, one group swerving to face the French foot as the other marched onwards towards the Swiss. The Gascons and the landsknechts came together with a great crash that brought down the entire front rank on each side — both had placed a rank of arquebusiers or pistoleers immediately behind the front rank of pikemen, and, at the moment of impact, each rank poured in a deadly volley. The second and third ranks, propelled forward by the men in their rear, met in a fierce 'push of pike', trampling on the corpses of their comrades. At this point the concealed Swiss in the French centre rose to their feet and rolled down the hillside in solid formation to crash into the column of landsknechts approaching them, so establishing a vast 'push of pike' along the entire centre of both armies. The final blow was supplied by de Boutieres' small force of gendarmerie charging into the flank of the landsknechts to send them reeling back down the hill. Supporting Spanish cavalry on the right of the landsknechts made a perfunctory move forward towards the Swiss flank, but recoiled from the pikes and rode to the rear, carrying the wounded del Vasto with them. The landsknechts, jammed together so that only their rear ranks were able to throw down their pikes and flee, were hacked down by the ruthless Swiss and the Gascons, losing 5,000 out of their original 7,000 men. At this disaster in the centre the Prince of Salerno marched his force off the field, accompanied by the survivors of the Florentine light horse.

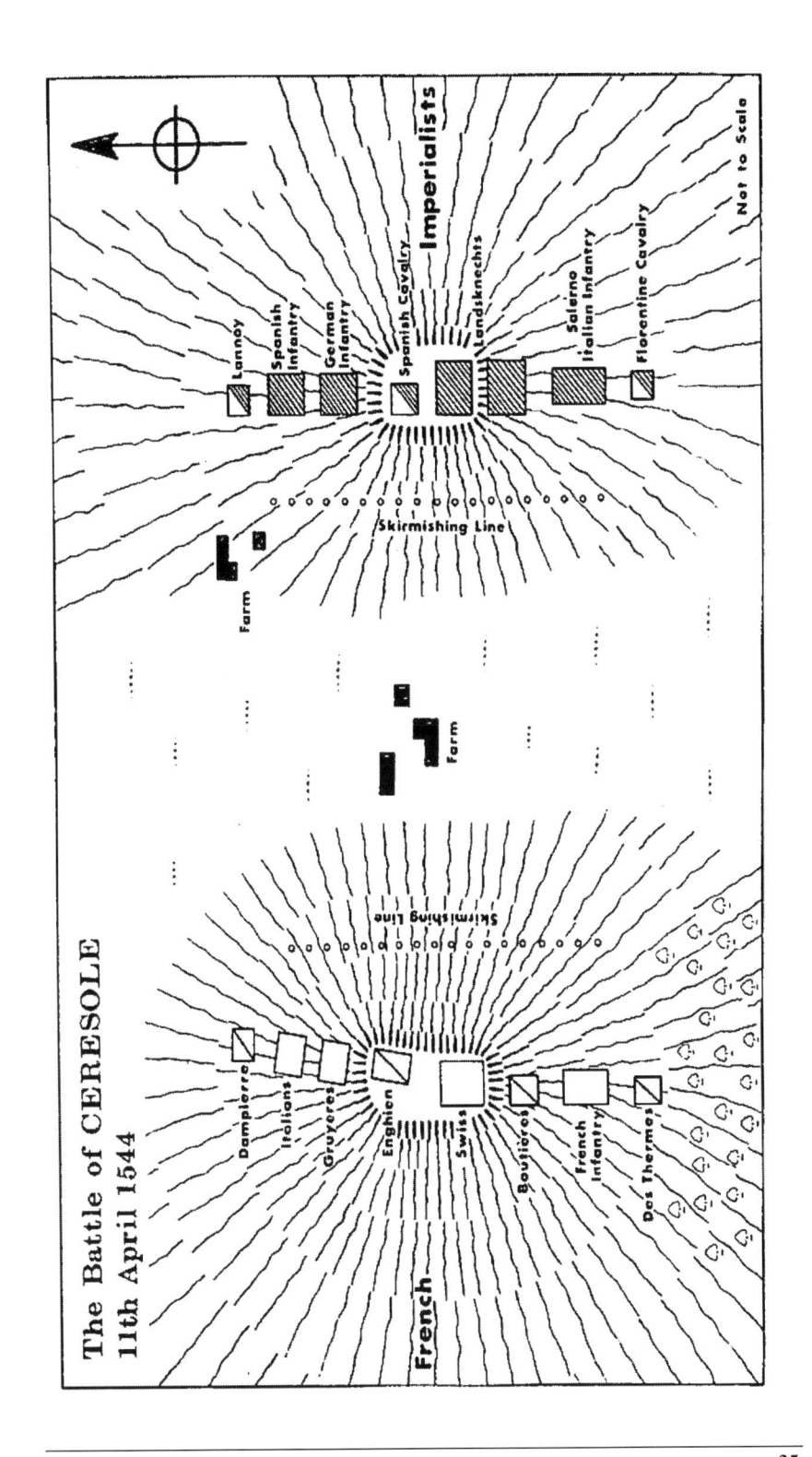

The Battle of CERESOLE
11th April 1544

The Imperialists' fortunes had prospered better at the other end of the battlefield, where Cardona's pike column of Spanish/German veterans, flanked by swarms of arquebusiers, had surged irresistibly forward against the infantry of Gruyeres and the Italians, who broke and fled without offering any serious resistance. Laying about them on all sides, the Imperialists pursued, oblivious of Lannoy's Neapolitan light horse on their right driven from the field by Dampierrc's cavalry.

Enghien, the French commander, seeing his left wing swept away while the Imperialist landsknecht column was still battling and was yet to be defeated in the centre, led his gendarmerie and the gentlemen volunteers against them, now well behind the French position. Halting, the Imperialists turned to receive the cavalry, whose first charge broke in a corner of their column, pushing right through to the rear, but at the cost of many casualties. The infantry closed ranks and their flanking arquebusiers poured in a heavy fire as Enghien's cavalry re-formed and made two more indecisive charges, the last being joined by Dampierre and the remnants of his light horse, who had returned from pursuing Lannoy's Neapolitans. The undulating ground separated this mêlée from the rest of the battle, and Enghien, who could not see what was happening elsewhere and now had less than 100 horsemen remaining, was full of despair when a courier galloped up with the news that the battle was won.

Cardona's infantry column, sensing defeat, began to retreat towards a wood in its rear, followed by Enghien and the survivors of his cavalry, reinforced by a newly arrived company of Italian horse — arquebusiers who, dismounting, firing and remounting, harassed the retreating column, slowing them up. The victorious Swiss and Gascons from the French centre re-formed as they ran side by side across the battlefield to join in the attack on the enemy columns, which were moving off under cover of salvoes of arquebus fire. It was the final blow to the outnumbered Imperialist infantry and, seeing the French cavalry preparing to charge, they threw down their pikes and surrendered.

Del Vasto lost this battle because both his wings were paralysed by cavalry charges, while the landsknechts in the centre, who might have held the Swiss, were outweighed by the Gascon foot, who themselves should have been contained by Salerno's Italians on the left wing. But they, in their turn, were affected by the inability of the Imperialist left-wing light horse to hold the cavalry of des Thermes. The Imperialist leader was wrong in his assumption that his considerable cavalry inferiority would be balanced by his superiority in arquebusiers, because the combination of enemy infantry and cavalry was too much for his unsupported infantry when deserted by their own cavalry.

Little quarter was given at Ceresole, the Imperialists losing 6,000 to 10,000 men against French losses of 1,500 to 2,000.

## Reconstructing the Battle as a Wargame
This stimulating set-piece battle is made more colourful by the fact that most of the various types of troops of the day took part, and these troops used the tactics and style of fighting of the period. Furthermore, the initial skirmishing by the arquebusiers is a wargame in itself and, forming an ideal curtain-raiser to the battle that follows, should be carried out on the slopes and in the valley between the ridges before bringing on the main bodies.

## Classification of Commanders
Both Enghien, the French commander, and del Vasto, the Imperialist leader, can hope for nothing better than an 'average' classification. Seemingly, having initially issued their orders, they allowed the course of the battle to slip away from them until Enghien, though with the bravest motives, detached himself from the main battle, and del Vasto was carried wounded from the scene of action. The Imperialist leader's supposition that the German infantry and arquebusiers would balance his lack of cavalry was not unreasonable, and has no bearing on his classification.

## Quality of Troops and Morale
The course of this battle indicates a distinct gulf in quality between various formations on both sides, who fall into two distinct types —the second-class troops such as the Florentine light horse, Salerno's Italian infantry, Gruyere's Swiss pikemen, the French/Italians, the Spanish cavalry and Lannoy's cavalry; and the first-class landsknechts, French/Swiss, Gascons and gentlemen volunteers. It is difficult to classify the artillery, for after an apparently indifferent and lengthy performance, it took no further part in the battle.

The undoubted affinity between the quality of the troops and their morale must be reflected by bestowing upon second-class troops a second-class morale status. All other troops were initially first-class. In the usual manner their morale rating will fluctuate during the course of the battle, according to combat circumstances.

## Effect and Construction of Terrain
There is a similarity between the two sides of the field, with both forces enjoying the early comforts of a ridge with elevated centre area. The restricted vision from the flanks caused by this higher section had no effect on the outcome of the battle, although, as evidenced by Enghien's ignorance of the course of the action, it could have made a real difference. There is no record of the farm buildings playing a particularly notable part in the action, but no doubt they will be a magnet to wargames' commanders, whose arquebusiers will skirmish actively in and around them.

This is a simple terrain to make. The two ridges may be represented by piles of books, wood blocks etc, placed along the entire length of each baseline, and a green cloth draped over the entire table so that it forms a valley in the centre.

**Military Possibilities**

The battle could have taken a different course in the following circumstances:

1. The Imperialist flanking cavalry had been better.

2. The landsknechts had held the Swiss, as they might have been expected to do.

3. Salerno's Italians had held and engaged the Gascon infantry, so protecting the landsknechts' flanks.

4. The Imperial left-wing horse had not been held by the opposing cavalry and not allowed to disrupt Salerno's Italians.

**Wargame Terrain for Ceresole**

*Imperialists*           *Gentle slope with high centre*

*French*               *Gentle slope with high centre*

*Note two small clusters of farm buildings*

# 5. The Battle of Pinkie 10 September 1547

LIKE MARIGNANO, Pinkie was a classic example of an old-fashioned infantry army being destroyed by a commander aware that cavalry and artillery were a deadly combination. The last tactical link in the long chain of battles where English combinations of weapons defeated the Scottish pike column, Pinkie was different in that it was won by horsemen and guns, and not by a combination of bowmen and dismounted men-at-arms as at Dupplin, Halidon Hill, Neville's Cross, Homildon and Flodden. It pointed the great lesson of warfare in this period — that cavalry could ride down musketeers who, in their turn, could mow down pikemen. To win battles a commander had to combine all his arms in the right proportion at the right place at the right time.

In September 1547 the Duke of Somerset, Lord Protector of England, marching parallel with Lord Clinton's fleet coasting along the shore, invaded Scotland with 16,000 men, about a quarter of them being cavalry, including foreign men-at-arms under Malatesta, 500 'Bulleners' (horsemen of the garrison of Boulogne), the Gentlemen Pensioners of the Royal Bodyguard, the Northern Horse (the 'Prickers' of the border marshes), and a troop of mounted arquebusiers under Pedro de Gamboa, a Spanish condottiere. Two of the foreign companies and 600 of the English infantry were armed with arquebuses, but the rest of the foot soldiers were the 'bows and bills' of the Flodden period.

Under the Regent Arran the Scots army of 23,000 men had only 1,500 Border 'Moss Troopers' as their cavalry arm, and the bulk of the infantry were traditional Scottish pikemen. They took up a defensive position west of the River Esk where it ran into the Firth of Forth between Musselburgh and Inveresk, their long line running from, the marsh on the river to the seashore, where guns were sited in an earthwork. It was a good unflankable position, protected by the sea on the north and on the south by the marsh, which could only be turned by a lengthy circular march over rough country. The River Esk was fordable in most places but, on the Scottish side, the steep and exposed slope of Edmonston Edge had to be climbed by attacking troops after fording the river. On the day before the battle English cavalry scouting inland fell in with the main body of Scottish horse, who were easily routed with heavy casualties by the stronger men-at-arms, and their morale greatly depressed.

Apparently inspired by the similarity of the Scots position to that of the Spaniards at Ravenna, Somerset determined to occupy the high knoll that projected almost into the Scottish lines, on which was built Inveresk church. He intended to plant all his heavy guns on it and sweep the Scottish line with flanking fire. So the English army began to march northward from its position on Fawside Brae, led by a body of light horse under Lord Ogle. The three infantry divisions — vaward,

The Battle of PINKIE
10th September 1547

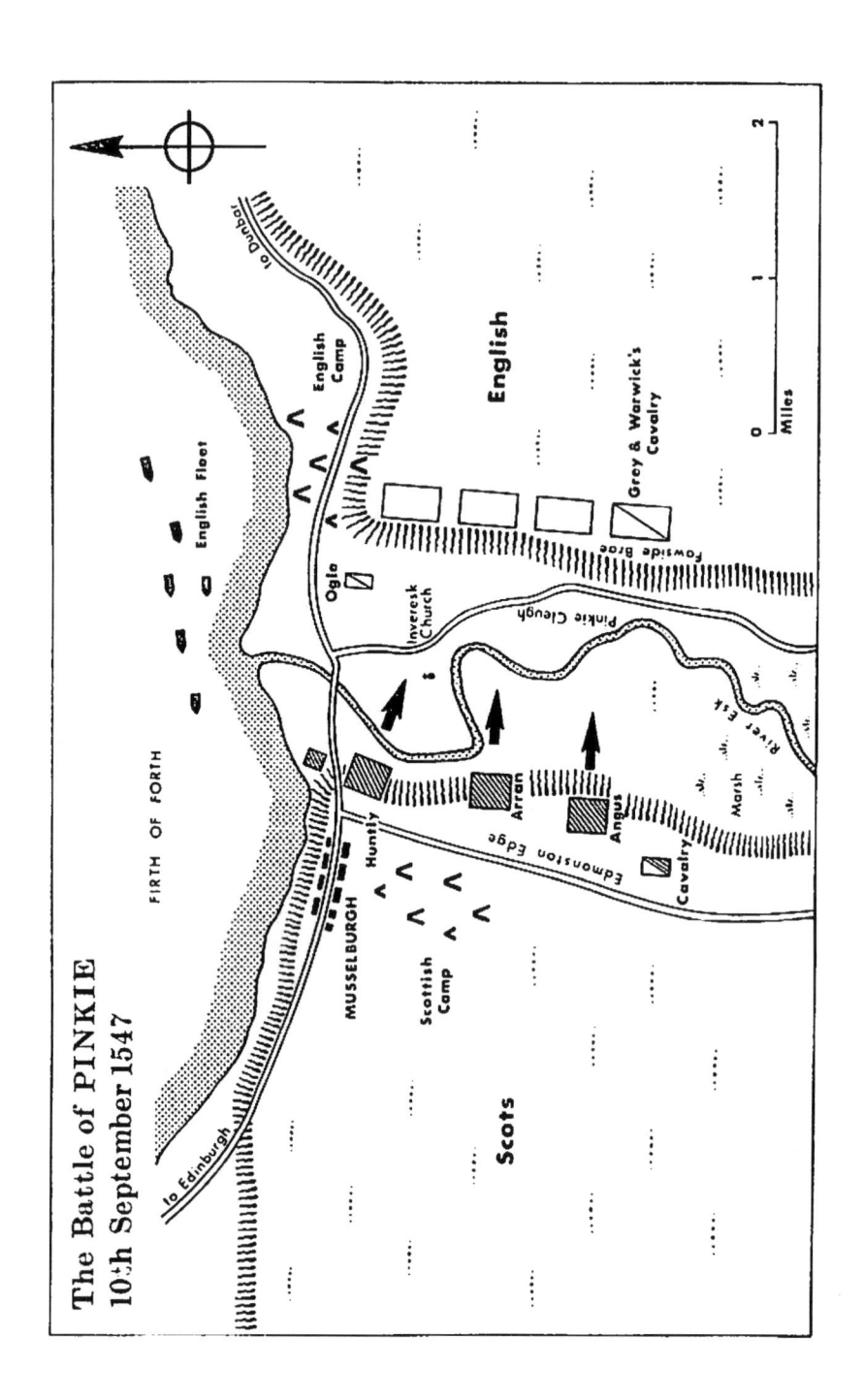

main-battle and rearward — followed, with the main body of cavalry and two heavy brigades making up the rear, and the guns spaced at intervals between the infantry divisions. Seeing the enemy moving towards the road that led to Dunbar and back to England, the Regent Arran incredibly surmised that they were about to retreat to Berwick, so he abandoned his intention of fighting the defensive battle for which his force was suited and ordered his men to leave their positions on Edmonston Edge, ford the River Esk and attack the English columns in flank as they moved across his front. In three columns of pikes the Scots came down the slope and across the river at the speed of horsemen rather than infantry. Their left wing under the Earl of Huntly was nearest the sea, flanked by a body of Highland bowmen; the centre, under Arran himself, included some artillery drawn by teams of men, and the vaward (right wing) under Angus had a few guns and the remains of the cavalry on its flank.

Greatly surprised by this unexpected Scottish move, Somerset hastily began to form 'front to flank' in a race against time: the arquebusiers and bowmen formed up on either flank of the billmen with some confusion and congestion in the centre as the guns were hastily pushed and pulled through the infantry, while the cavalry disposed themselves on the wings. Suddenly, as the tightly packed ranks of the Scottish left wing were crossing the river between the Inveresk knoll and the sea, they were hit by a broadside from the guns of the fleet lying offshore, completely dispersing the Highland archers on Huntly's flank, who fled in panic from the scene. The hissing roundshot from the ships' guns also ploughed into the mass of pikemen, causing heavy casualties, so that Huntly hastily shifted the disordered column inland out of range, where it coalesced with Arran's main-battle into one great mass.

Unchecked by this reverse, although delayed by the difficulties of manhauling their guns across rough country, the Scottish columns splashed through the river and across the flat land beyond before ascending the slope to the crest where the English, now almost in battle order, awaited their onslaught. As Arran's 4 guns fell in on Huntly's left, the line re-formed, but the Scottish cavalry, still smarting from their rough handling of the previous day, hung back in echelon far to the right rear. This fact, with the disappearance of the light infantry archers, transformed the Scottish army into a great mass of pikes with totally unprotected flanks.

Somerset was a good enough commander to seize the opportunity of halting the infantry by successive cavalry charges, while his artillery and missile-armed infantry poured a destructive fire into their flanks. The cavalry began their attacks when the Scots were halfway up the slope of Fawside Brae, amid the fields of Pinkie Clough, in an area of newly reaped stubble and low earth banks that hindered neither cavalry nor infantry. In went the 'Bulleners' and the 'Bands' of Grey, Norwich and Somerset— 1,800 horsemen striking into Huntly on the flank of the Scottish column. A contemporary chronicler records:

'The Scots stood at defence, shoulders nigh together, the fore-rank stooping low before, their fellows behind holding their pikes in both hands, the one end of the pike against the right foot, the other against the enemy's breast, so nigh as place and space might suffer. So thick were they that a bare finger should as easily pierce through the bristles of a hedgehog as any man encounter the front of pikes.'

Although charging courageously, the English horsemen were thrown back with relative ease, leaving great heaps of dead men and horses only 6 feet from the Scottish line. Intent on halting the Scots until his guns were in position, Somerset sent in a second cavalry charge against the Scottish main-battle, the 1,600 horsemen including the Gentlemen Pensioners (the Royal Bodyguard), Vane's Band and the demi-lances of Lord Fitzwalter. Like the first, this attack was beaten off with great loss, some leaders being lost and several standards put in jeopardy. By now the Earl of Warwick had positioned the guns of the English right wing and centre to bear upon the Scottish left (Huntly's division and parts of Angus's). Dramatically the elation of the hitherto triumphant pikemen was dashed by hails of roundshot fired into their close-packed ranks from less than 300 yards. At the same time arquebusiers and bowmen swarmed forward to fire into the stationary columns, while the horse-arquebusiers of the mercenary de Gamboa gave an exhibition of Continental tactics by caracoling across the front of the helpless pikemen.

Hemmed in by heaps of dead men and horses, their ranks forced into a disordered and restricted mass by the cavalry charges, the Scots infantry was quite incapable of preventing itself from being shattered by weight of fire. With the cry 'Betrayed!' the Regent Arran galloped from the field. Left to carry on as best they could, his commanders took hasty uncoordinated action. On the right Angus felt that it was essential to retire out of range of the guns. Trying to do this by falling back down the hillside, his retreat quickly turned into a rout as the disordered and now panicking pikemen cast down their pikes and fled instead of re-forming at the foot of the hill. Seeing this, the whole Scots line followed, and with Huntly's force, which had taken most punishment, all streamed off in a general stampede. The English cavalry charged again, to ride down and butcher the fleeing infantry as the Scots horsemen, who had never closed, rode away without loss. The Scots lost 10,000 to 14,000 men against English losses of about 250, mostly cavalry, for their infantry was hardly engaged.

**Reconstructing the Battle as a Wargame**
Lay out Somerset's force 12 inches south of the knoll, with only his right wing facing the church, and Arran's in its historical dispositions 12 inches from his baseline. The wargamer playing Somerset, who has been given written details of Somerset's original intentions, occupies the first game-move by marching diagonally north-west into Pinkie

Cleugh, towards the knoll. The 'Regent Arran' then takes one-third of the first game-move to assess the situation, leaving him two-thirds of the move in which to take action. He decides to attack and the Scots move forward 'at charge speed' for the remainder of game-move No 1. Obviously their guns move more slowly, but should still be allowed a faster move-distance than usual.

Seeing the Scots begin their attack, 'Somerset' takes one-third of the second game-move to react. At this point, to simulate his tactical superiority, he is given a brief note of the real-life tactics employed by his namesake. Although not compelled to follow these historical dictates, he might do well to follow them as they were successful and probably the very best tactics under the circumstances. Thus 'Somerset' has two-thirds of the second game-move to react to 'Arran's' unexpected charge and, if the game is to authentically simulate the events of 1547, it becomes a race as 'Somerset's' force endeavours to turn and take up defensive positions before being hit by the onrushing Scottish pikemen. If these conditions are followed, it is likely that the battle will proceed much as it did in real life.

During this the second game-move Huntly, on the Scottish left, should edge slightly north-east as if to bar the road on which it is thought that Somerset intends to withdraw. Then, at the end of the game-move, the guns of the English fleet, off-table but just within range of the beach, fire on Huntly and the archers, who react in accordance with the rules.

### Classification of Commanders

The Lord Protector Somerset must be classified as an 'above average' commander, whereas the Regent Arran cannot rate any higher than 'average' and may well be considered 'below average'. Arran's abysmal tactics and the effect of the heavy English firepower may well be too much for the Scots, so that this wargame battle becomes impracticable. One may simulate English superiority by the ploy of revealing to the wargamer 'Somerset' the historically successful tactics employed by the Lord Protector.

### Quality of Troops and Morale

With the exception of the Scottish horse (who have second-class morale throughout), all the troops began with a first-class morale rating, which fluctuated according to the course of the battle. The Scottish pikemen should be given a higher points value when mêléeing if they are reasonably to simulate the doughty deeds of the day.

### Effect and Construction of Terrain

While the terrain had a bearing on events and the subsequent outcome of the battle, it had no real effect upon tactics, with the possible exception of the fleet on the adjacent sea. The River Esk was wadable and it is unlikely that the slope of the Fawside Brae impeded the headlong onslaught of the Scots.

The terrain is interesting to construct, with high ground on both sides, leaving sufficient space on the English side for their historical dispositions. It can be made by using 'long runs' of hills, either prefabricated terrain features laid on the table top or by stretching a cloth over books, boxes, boards etc, placed to provide the correct contours. The sea and the fleet will be 'off-table'.

**Military Possibilities**

Had the Scots remained in their defensive positions, would the result have been different or would there have been another Ravenna?

If the Scottish horse had not been beaten on the previous day, to the detriment of their morale, would their presence on the field have provided the much needed Scottish flank protection? Perhaps their numbers were too small to be effective anyway.

All guns on both sides were manhandled, and the wargamer is reminded that the sole firepower of the Scots was limited to the few guns with Arran and Angus. Finally, what happened to the Scottish guns in the beach earthwork?

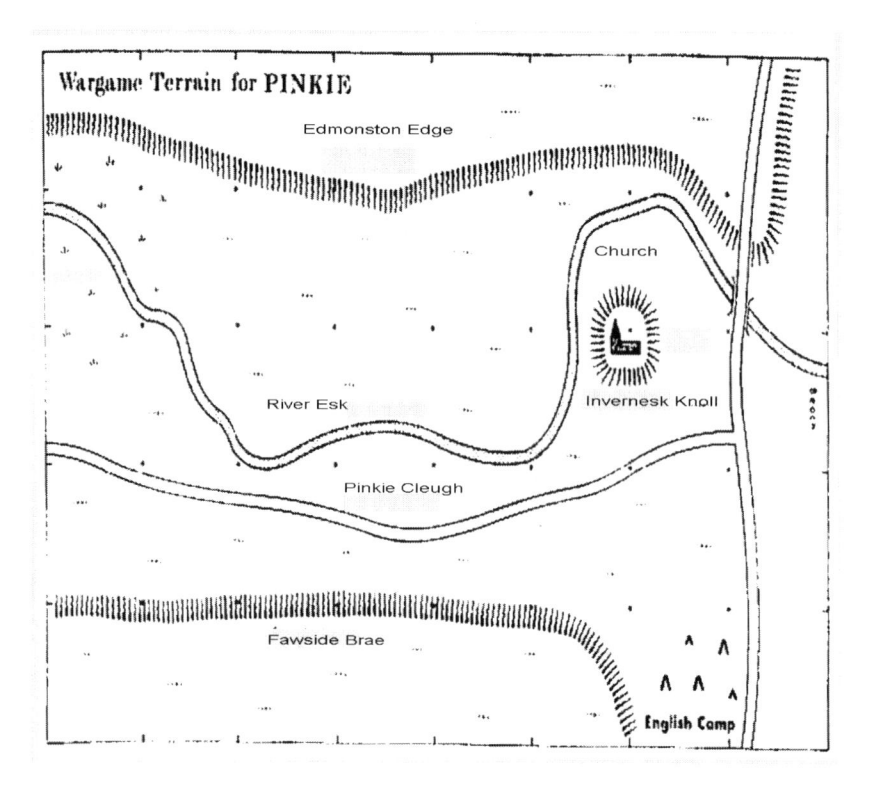

# 6. The Battle of Dreux 19 December 1562

CONDE AND Coligny, marching their Huguenot army towards Dreux on the morning of 19 December, reached an area between the villages of Epinay and Blainville to find the Catholic army positioned across their route. Having neglected to put out scouts, they were completely surprised. They had forewarned the enemy of their approach by the sound of their drums, and the Catholics, commanded by the shrewd seventy-year-old Constable Montmorency, were formed in a single line some 2,500 yards long across the road to Dreux, with their right wing resting on Epinay and their left on Blainville, two villages protected by thick woods and rivers, so that they could not be turned. Personally leading the 'main-battle', Montmorency had divided his army into two instead of the usual three divisions, with the Marshal St Andre commanding the right. The Duc de Guise, although probably the greater captain, was serving in Andre's division at the head of his own double strength *compagnie d'ordonnance*.

With 4 guns in front of Epinay and another 4 across the road just west of Blainville, the Constable's troops occupied the space between the two villages. Sansac, commanding 8 companies of light horse (400 men), was on the extreme left, and the Constable himself, with 18 *compagnies d'ordonnance* (2,500 cavalry and retainers), lay next to the barricaded village of Blainville and the guns. To the right of the Constable's men stood 20 companies of French infantry (4,000 men) from Picardy and Brittany, and in the centre the solid phalanx of 28 companies of Swiss pikemen (5,600 men). Andre's division continued the line to the right with 3 companies (each 50 lances) of gendarmerie under Damville, the Constable's son; then came 10 *enseignes* (companies) of German landsknechts (2,000 men), and 20 *enseignes* (each 200 men) of French infantry, mainly from the 'Old Bands' of Piedmonte. St Andre lay slightly ahead of the latter with 12 companies (each 50 lances) of gendarmerie, and on the extreme right were 14 companies of Spanish infantry (4,800 men). The greater part of St Andre's 'vaward' was screened by the houses of Epinay and by the wood; the cavalry were dismounted and the infantry had their pikes lowered so that they were hardly visible. St Andre's 14 guns were placed east of Epinay, bearing on the road. The Duc de Guise held 200 horse (including some noblemen volunteers) in reserve behind the village. The total Catholic army comprised 3,000 cavalry and 16,000 infantry.

The light horse that headed the Huguenot column of route came under fire from the Constable's artillery as soon as they appeared, and the leading squadrons were forced to seek the shelter of a dip in the ground. Conde and the Admiral Coligny rode out in front of their halted army to view the partly screened Catholic position. Sure that the Catholics would not leave their defended position, Coligny advised that the Huguenots should turn westward and march up the Treon Road to

The Battle of DREUX
19th December 1562

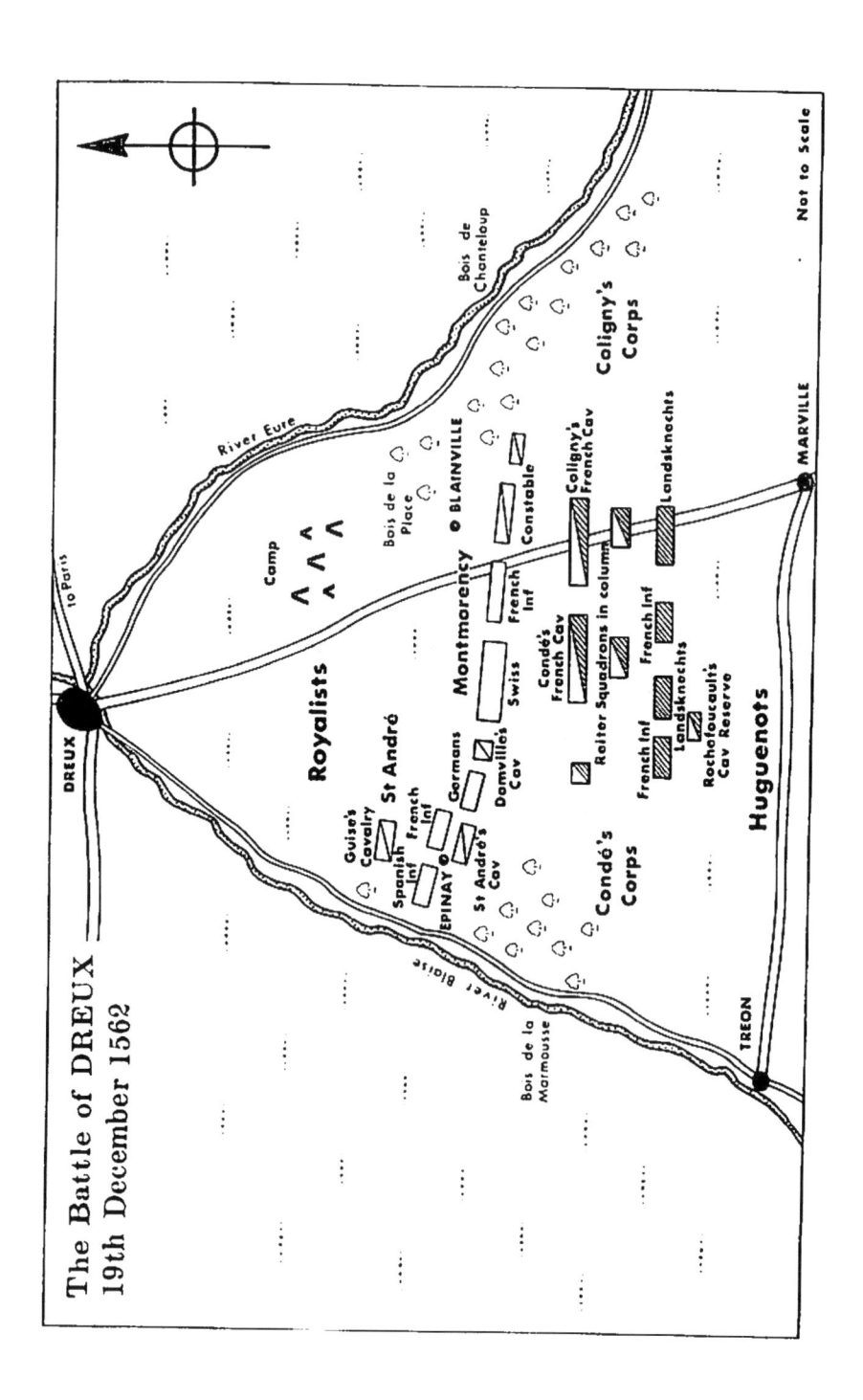

avoid a general action, so the baggage and all the guns save 5 light field pieces set off in this direction. At the same time the Huguenots deployed from column of march to a fighting front in case the Catholics made a sudden attack on the exposed flank of their army moving across its front. They deployed in two divisions but with a second line and reserves; facing Montmorency was Coligny with the 'vaward' consisting of 400 French heavy cavalry, 4 companies of German Reiters (about 1,000 pistoleers), then 11 *enseignes* of French and 6 of German landsknechts (some 3,500 foot). On his left, facing the eastern third of St Andre's division, was Conde with the 'main-battle', comprising 500 gendarmes, 6 companies of Reiters (1,300 men), 400 argoulets (light cavalry) and horse arquebusiers, and 12 *enseignes* of French and 6 of German landsknechts (some 4,000 foot soldiers). The total strength of the force was about 4,000 horse and 8-9,000 foot.

The two armies in battle order faced each other a mile apart for about two hours, until at noon Conde, believing that the Constable would not leave his defensive position, decided to follow the artillery and baggage moving westward to the Treon Road. The Huguenots had barely begun to move when the Constable's line started to come downhill to fall upon their flank, so Conde faced his army to the front again and began the general advance that had been his original intention. The Huguenots attacked in two lines, an unusual formation for the day, with French cavalry in front and Reiters in support, followed by infantry, with a small cavalry reserve of 100 lances. Conde did not move against the fortified village of Epinay or the artillery alongside it, but masked the area with the infantry of his column and two squadrons of Reiters.

In the eastern half of the field towards Blainville the Huguenot attack was completely successful as Coligny's French horse, supported by his Reiters, rode down the lesser numbers of the Constable's cavalry. In spite of his seventy years the old man fought in the front line and was captured. In the fashion of the time the Admiral's cavalry got out of hand and pursued the flying Catholics, so it was some time before Coligny could rally sufficient men to move across to the other wing of the field, but his 3,000 infantry played a small part in defeating the Constable's company of French foot, and apparently remained in much the same place throughout the battle. The gendarmerie, under the Prince of Porcien, completely routed the French infantry and Sansac's light horse in and around Blainville, to capture the village and the guns in front of it.

Things had gone very differently on the western side of the battlefield, where Conde attacked the Swiss, the best soldiers in the Catholic army, with all his troops but a small infantry group and two Reiter squadrons remaining opposite the Catholic left wing. At first Conde's attack went well as the gendarme companies of De Muy and Araret carved their way right through the Swiss formation to come out on the other side — but without causing it to break up. Then the main body of Huguenot horse, French and Reiters, charged the Swiss in flank and pushed them back, so that they left the guns they were guarding. But still they refused to break, although falling back towards St Andre's line. He sent 3 companies of his gendarmerie to their aid, but they were routed by 2 squadrons of Reiters, their survivors falling back and rallying on Guise's small cavalry reserve. Determined to smash the stubborn Swiss, Conde withdrew the 6 landsknecht foot companies facing St Andre's front and threw them in, but the Swiss, seeing their old enemy in front of them, advanced and easily drove them from the field. In desperation Conde then sent forward the last of his cavalry, the 100 lances held in reserve, but they too were repulsed, and the frustrated Huguenot units fell back from the battered but triumphant Swiss pike phalanx.

Knowing that the last of the Huguenot cavalry had been used up. Guise at the head of 200 gendarmes led by 500 arquebusiers, and with the Spanish infantry and the French 'Old Bands' infantry, came out of the woods in front of Epinay to attack the Huguenot line at a point where the only opposition was a Reiter squadron and two squares of raw French infantry who, attacked by both foot and horse, broke at once. Simultaneously St Andre charged out with what he had left of his cavalry and ten companies of Catholic landsknechts and, with Guise's force, fell upon the German infantry who had just been beaten off by the Swiss. Said to have been 'the most cowardly lot of landsknechts who had come into France during the forty years of war', the Germans threw up their pikes and surrendered. The disordered, exhausted squadrons of Conde's gendarmes and Reiters, dispirited at the collapse of their infantry, began to leave the field, and Conde, after vainly trying to rally them, charged into the Catholic mass at the head of a handful of horsemen and was captured.

The battle died down, and Andre and Guise believed it to be over until, through the December dusk, they saw coming upon them from the south a large body whose white scarves revealed that they were Coligny's cavalry from the other wing. The Admiral had rallied about 1,000 Reiters and 300 gendarmes and formed them in three troops. Guise and St Andre, taken somewhat by surprise, formed a new front in and about Epinay, where confused but fierce fighting was still going on when darkness fell. The Huguenots rode down the Catholic horse and captured St Andre, who was almost immediately killed by a man who bore him a grudge. Hard as they fought, however, the newly arrived Huguenot cavalry were unable to defeat the Catholic infantry, who resisted stoutly from houses and trees; and after many attempts to dislodge them, Coligny withdrew in good order, with two of the five Huguenot guns, to a camp three miles from the battlefield, where he was joined by the remnants of his infantry.

An indecisive battle where each side lost between 3,000 and 4,000 men, including prisoners, Dreux was notable in that day and age for:
(a) the incredible failure of an army with superior cavalry not knowing that the enemy were within a day's march of them,
(b) a lack of preliminary skirmishing,
(c) the remarkable generalship displayed by Guise in holding back until Conde's horse were exhausted,

(d) the battle's duration of five hours instead of the usual short sharp clash,
(e) the capture of both commanders-in-chief,
(f) the fact that steady infantry can win a battle without being able to exploit their victory if the enemy still has in the field a superior cavalry force that can block pursuit,
(g) the fact that the defeated army retreated without pursuit and in good order, and
(h) showing that simple linear tactics are always dangerous and reserves of both arms should always be kept.

### Reconstructing the Battle as a Wargame

Set up the game with the Catholics in position, or, without the Huguenot commander being aware of the enemy's dispositions, march the Huguenots on to the table and then, when their leading troops are fired upon, set up the Catholic forces. At this stage the Huguenots will be laid out in their historical dispositions.

On their right the Huguenot cavalry (presumably powerful, heavy cavalry will defeat lighter cavalry and lower-rated infantry) must get out of hand, which can be simulated by the 'two-move' contact rule. Conde must not be allowed to attack the Swiss en masse or in any manner other than in the authentic historical order. Coligny's late arriving cavalry should have a high morale, resulting from their successes on the right flank.

The course of the battle can be programmed as follows:

| RIGHT | LEFT |
| --- | --- |
| 1 Coligny's cavalry successfully attacks Blainville. | Conde, after masking Epinay, attacks the Swiss, and his troops in succession are soundly beaten. |
| 2 Coligny's cavalry pursues, but his infantry stays put. | Conde's masking force is routed by Guise, as St Andre routs the remainder of Conde's force. Conde is captured. |
| 3 Coligny's cavalry arrives on the left | — to ride down Catholic horse and capture St Andre, but fail to dislodge infantry from Epinay and the woods. |

### Classification of Commanders

It would seem reasonable to classify the Huguenot commanders Conde and Coligny as 'average', with the same rating for Montmorency, St Andre and the Duc de Guise, the Catholic leaders. Guise may have displayed good tactics by not attacking Conde earlier, but that might have been through hesitancy. Anyway, he did not pursue, and nothing else he did in this battle indicates that he was above average on the day.

### Quality of Troops

The Swiss on the Catholic side must undoubtedly be classified as elite troops. For the Huguenots, Porcien's gendarmerie

might be given a similar classification. Most of the other troops are 'average', but the following should be rated as second-class:
French infantry in the Blainville area.
The Huguenot landsknechts.
The raw French/Huguenot infantry in front of Epinay.

## Morale
All the troops started this battle with first-class morale status, but that remained steady or fell according to events.

Unless 'weighted', few wargames rules will allow the Swiss pikemen to perform so valiantly. To simulate their gallant deeds, their morale rating should be given elite status (by adding at least 1 to each morale dice throw).

## Effect and Construction of Terrain
The villages played an important part in the battle, particularly Epinay, which, together with the wood on that flank, provided concealment for Andre's Catholic forces during the early part of the battle. Otherwise the battle area was flat and suitable for all arms.

When constructing this terrain, the villages and the woods should be of a 'nominal' nature, the villages represented by a closely grouped cluster of three or four houses and the woods by a few trees dotted here and there on a different coloured base whose area denotes the wood's extent. This 'nominal' construction facilitates the handling of troops in table-top wargames.

## Military Possibilities
The course of the battle might have altered had the Huguenots not sent away nearly all their guns before the action began. In fact, if they had employed scouts in the normally accepted military fashion, they would not have been surprised, and/or the Catholics might have lacked the time to take up their positions. In either case the battle could have taken a different course, or even not have occurred at all.

If Coligny had managed to rally his cavalry more quickly and join Conde, the latter might have been more successful. His success would have depended on the Swiss breaking, but as their dogged defence was the key to the battle, historical authenticity would then go by the board.

In the last stages of the battle Coligny's cavalry unsuccessfully tried to push the Catholic infantry out of Epinay. Had they done so, it might not have made much difference, as the coming of night would probably have persuaded Coligny to retire to camp, as he did in reality. Had Guise, at an earlier stage, come out of the wood to attack in front of Epinay, he might either (a) have been more successful and brought about a Catholic victory, or (b) attacked prematurely and been defeated, resulting in a Huguenot triumph.

If the battle is to be authentic, the Swiss must be able to hold out, as this is the key to the whole conflict. To enable them to do this, their morale rating should be almost unshakable.

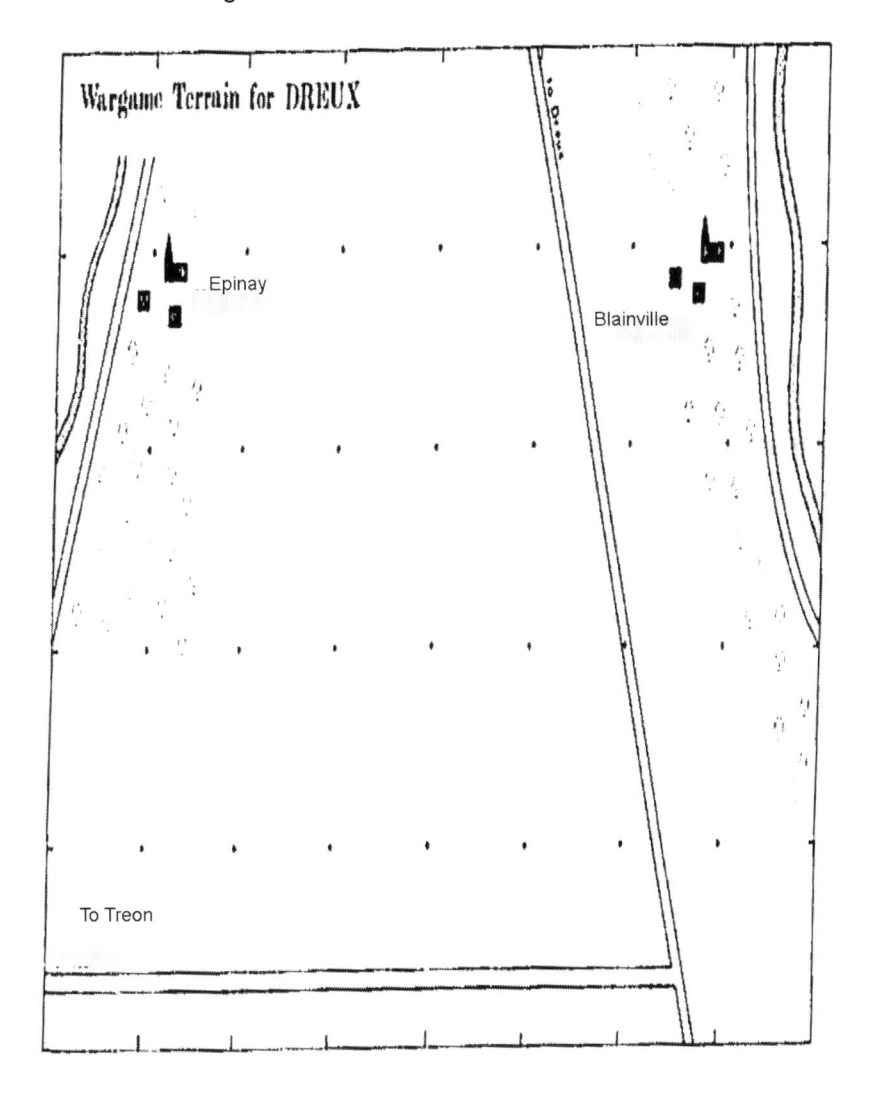

**Wargame Terrain for DREUX**

Epinay

Blainville

to Dreux

To Treon

# 7. The Battle of Coutras 20 October 1587

THE HUGUENOT leader, Henry of Navarre, and his cousin Conde, had gathered together a small army of formidable veterans, their arquebusiers mounted on a motley assortment of horses to keep up with the cavalry, and were marching south towards a much larger Royalist army under the King of France's favourite, Joyeuse. When the strong Huguenot cavalry vanguard led by La Tremouille vanquished a similar scouting force of Mercurio's stradiots in a dusk skirmish through the long main street of Coutras, Joyeuse halted his army ten miles from the town. Henry took up a position in ideal defensive ground, 700 yards wide, with woods backed by rivers on each flank — if he was defeated, the lack of exits would make the position a death-trap.

Joyeuse marched at midnight but did not achieve surprise, as the 200 light horse and 80 men-at-arms sent out by Henry to patrol the road engaged in a running fight with the same stradiots who had been bested on the previous night and with 400 gendarmes. They were slowly driven back towards Coutras, the heavy arquebus fire warning Henry of the approach of the Royalists. Joyeuse's long column came on the scene in early daylight and wheeled from line of march into line of battle. The weary army took until 9am to position itself, with infantry on the wings and cavalry in the centre on open ground to the left of the high road. On the left were two very strong infantry regiments — one of them the 'old Picardie', the senior infantry corps of the French Army, and the other Tiercellin — totalling 1,000 pikes and 1,800 arquebuses, so that each was twice as big as the small Huguenot regiments. In the centre were Mercurio's stradiots, several bands of light horse and 500 lances under Montigny. The ground to their right was occupied by the rest of the gendarmerie companies, some 1,200 lances in a long line; the front rank consisted entirely of 'great lords', with Joyeuse's personal company and his banner in the centre. On the extreme right of the cavalry stood the infantry regiments of Cluseau and Verduisant — some 2,500 men — with a scattering of mounted arquebusiers between them and the Pallard Marsh.

Henry's men had all slept comfortably in Coutras and were fresh. The right of the line was held by three foot regiments (2,000 men) in the Warren, a ditch-bordered enclosure of low shrubs from which they would only be dislodged by first-class infantry, as it was unsuitable ground for cavalry. On their left, stretching as far as the high road, stood five bodies of cavalry. Those who had been skirmishing before dawn, supported by Gascon and Poitevin horse under La Tremouille and Turenne (about 400 in all), were placed nearest the infantry, and then came 600 cuirassiers in two columns, 50 men wide by 6 deep, under Conde and Henry. The former commanded the right of the battle and the latter the left. Soissons, with a column of 200 Northern horse, was to their left. The interval between each cavalry block was occupied

53

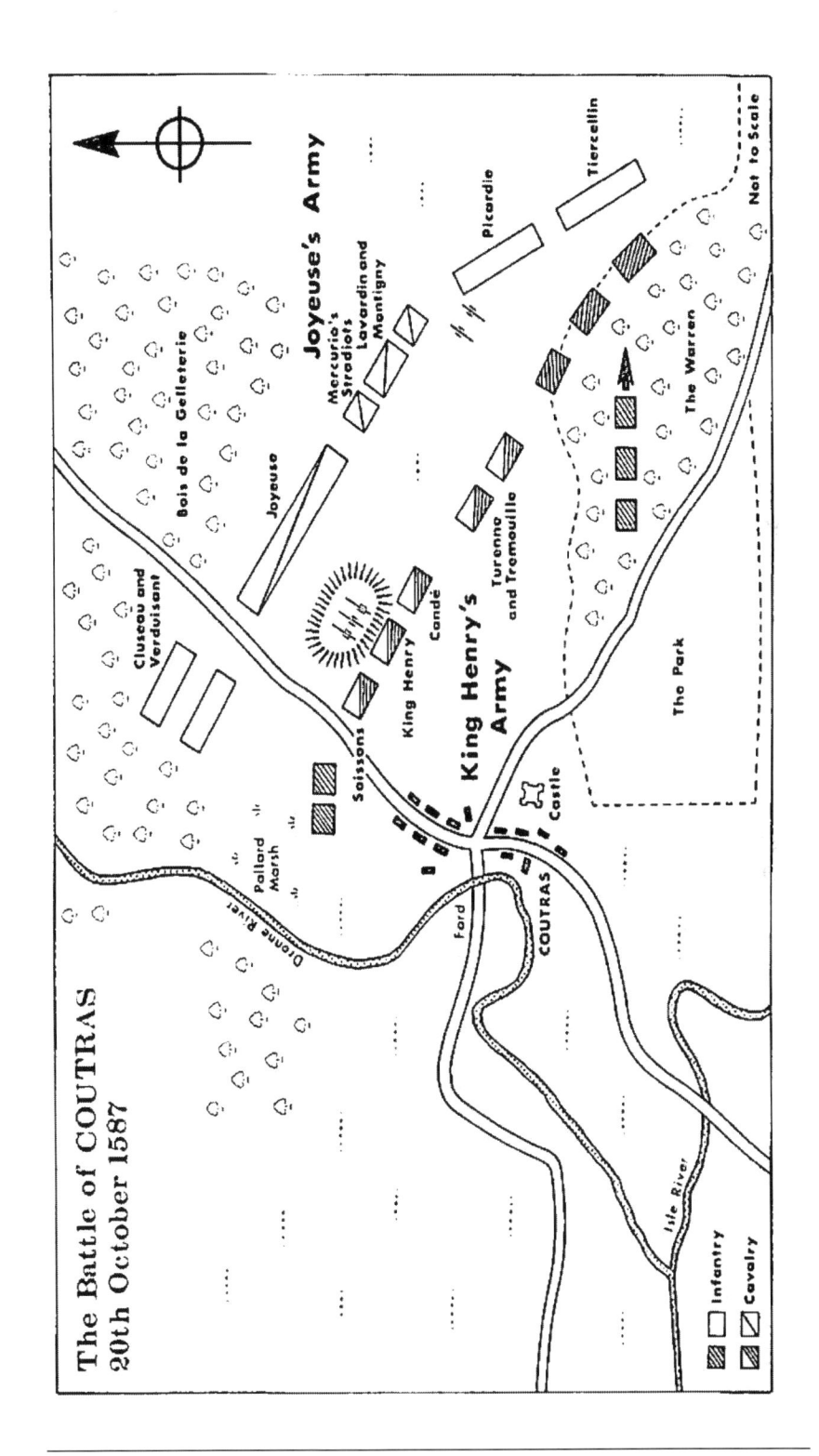

by *enfants perdus*—detachments of arquebusiers five deep, the front rank kneeling. They had been strictly enjoined not to fire until the enemy came within twenty yards of them, so that they would not be ridden down. Henry intended to receive the charge and only to strike himself when the enemy, shaken by musketry, would be close and in a state of confusion.

Just before the battle began, Henry received the reinforcement of three guns brought by his gunnery specialist, Clermont d'Amboise, escorted by three foot regiments, sent to reinforce the Warren. The guns were positioned on a mound to the right of Soissons's cavalry. The left flank was held by *enfants perdus* and 300 arquebusiers detached from the regiments in the Warren.

The Huguenot force totalled 5,000 infantry, 1,300 cavalry and 3 guns against the Catholics' 2,000 horse, 8,000 infantry and 2 guns.

Not allowing the latter to settle down, Henry ordered Clermont d'Amboise to take some long shots at them. The first ball knocked over Joyeuse's personal banner and others carved bloody lanes in the flank of an infantry regiment. The return fire from the enemy guns, placed ineffectively in low-lying ground, did little damage, and, smarting under the galling fire, the Catholic line moved forward. At the eastern end of the battlefield their infantry engaged the Huguenots in the Warren but made little impression, while on the extreme left of the Huguenot line the detached arquebusiers, far from just containing the enemy, as they had been ordered, charged into the wood and pushed back the Catholic pikemen; the fierce struggle that developed here was still going on when the battle had been won and lost elsewhere. But the first clash of horse in the centre saw Montigny's gendarmes, the light horse and Mercurio's stradiots, attack the smaller numbers of La Tremouille and Turenne with such vigour that the routed Huguenot horsemen fled in a confused mass past the corner of the Warren as far as the first houses of Coutras. After some sprawling confused fighting, with some of the Huguenot fugitives swimming the river to escape, La Tremouille and Turenne, with a handful of survivors, managed to join Conde's corps.

This Catholic success was of little avail, for the decisive action was taking place in the centre, as Henry of Navarre intended. Joyeuse charged so early with his 1,200 horsemen that their line became ragged and gaps appeared in it. When the cavalry were only twenty yards from the five-deep formations of *enfants perdus,* the latter fired a great volley that brought down scores of men and horses. Then the reeling horsemen were hit by the six-deep blocks of the Huguenot squadrons charging in at the trot, which took them right through the Catholic line at every point. In five minutes Joyeuse's battle line had melted away as panic-stricken fugitives rode for their lives in all directions. In this attack Henry performed valiantly but Conde was unhorsed. With no enemy left to attack, some of the victorious Huguenot horsemen turned to cut up the flank of the Picardie regiment, which was frontally engaged along the edge of the Warren.

Seeing the disaster in the centre and lacking any reserve, the entire Catholic army broke and fled, many being cut down, including Joyeuse himself, in the slaughter of 400 nobility and 3,000 lower ranks before quarter was granted. The Huguenot losses were less than 200.

Tactically, Coutras answered the question of the relative values of shallow and deep cavalry formations.

### Reconstructing the Battle as a Wargame

The preliminary cavalry skirmish in Coutras can be utilised to decide the amount of time Henry has to make his dispositions, while determining how quickly Joyeuse appears. Alternatively, the wargame can begin with Henry forming up as he did historically, and Joyeuse following suit.

The Huguenot artillery arrived late on the scene, and its time of arrival can be determined by the use of Chance Cards. In any event, if historical authenticity is to be achieved, Clermont d'Amboise's guns must be allowed to arrive in time to open fire upon the Catholics, because it was this unremitting fire that goaded the latter into a premature attack.

The two Catholic guns start the game in low-lying ground, where they are relatively ineffective; but the 'Catholic' wargamer is free to do as he wishes with his own two pieces from the moment the Huguenot artillery opens fire.

The Battle of Coutras can be divided into four separate but simultaneous engagements:
1  On the left in the woods.
2  In the centre/right between the cavalry.
3  On the right at the Warren.
4  In the centre between the arquebusiers and the cavalry.

Separate engagements often occur during the course of a battle; each one here, though self-contained, is an integral part of the battle. Unconnected actions on the wargames table can be simulated in a novel way by setting up four small terrains in different parts of the room or house. On each of them the wargamers commanding that particular sector of the battle fight it out, and the results of each are collated at the end to determine the overall decision.

### Classification of Commanders

Henry was an 'above average' commander, whereas Joyeuse, a Court favourite, cannot be rated higher than 'below average'. However realistic these ratings may be, they may distort the course of the wargame so that it veers away from historical authenticity. As in the case of Pinkie, this can be remedied by presenting the 'Huguenot' commander with written details of Henry's successful tactics, with strong suggestions that they are followed!

### Quality of Troops
The Huguenots were so superior in most aspects of this battle that they might well rate an 'elite' classification as against the Catholics' 'average' rating. Even the reverse suffered by the cavalry of La Tremouille and Turenne could be attributable to their lesser numbers.

Rather than starting this wargame with the 'Catholic' commander labouring under a sense of grievance because his troops are of lower rating than the enemy, initially he can be left in blissful ignorance of that fact. The situation can best be handled by beginning the battle with both sides of level rating, but through the factor of fatigue (most marked at Coutras), the Catholics' fighting qualities and stamina steadily diminish as each game-move unreels. This can be simulated by allowing the first three game-moves to pass normally, the next three to bring a 1 point deduction from all Catholic dice throws, the next three game-moves (7, 8 and 9) a 2 points deduction, and so on.

### Morale
All the troops are first-class at the start of the battle, their morale fluctuating in accordance with the course of the combat.

The sole exception may well be the *enfants perdus,* those brave Huguenot arquebusiers, who showed exceptional qualities to stand and hold their fire until the charging cavalry were only twenty yards away. This advantage for the Huguenots may be simulated by adding a bonus to all their dice throws concerned with morale.

### Effects and Construction of Terrain
The Huguenot position was ideal for their defensive tactics, with the Warren as the key position. They found a convenient mound on which to place their artillery, whereas the Catholics, through lack of foresight or just sheer bad tactics, sited theirs in low ground. The river near the Huguenot baseline is obviously uncrossable except at the bridges and one ford, and it is here that the fleeing Huguenot cavalry were trapped and will suffer accordingly.

It is a pleasant terrain to construct and presents no particular difficulties.

### Military Possibilities
In this battle the only success gained by the Catholics was their cavalry's rout of the numerically inferior force of horse led by La Tremouille and Turenne. Had these successful Catholic cavalry not pursued so far, but rallied and re-formed before reaching the river, they might have turned into the Huguenot's rear with devastating effect. They could not turn left into the Warren, however, and by the time they had rallied Henry and his *enfants perdus* would have defeated the impetuously charging Joyeuse and been ready for them. The victorious Catholic cavalry at the river had no real time to do anything and, although this is not recorded, they probably retreated by a convenient road when the Catholic army broke up.

An interesting and effective simulation of the manner in which cavalry got out of hand when pursuing (it happened in all ages — Prince Rupert's horsemen and Wellington's cavalry in the Peninsular War were noted for it) is by 'two-move contact'. When a cavalry force come into a mêlée, it is obliged to remain in contact with the enemy for the next two game-moves. This means that if the enemy is routed and flees back a charge-move, the victorious cavalry pursues them (enjoying a 'free' hack at their backs) for the next two moves. This simulates a wild pursuit while producing the reasonable situation of defeated cavalry rarely being able to rally, and ends with the victorious horsemen having to make their way back to their own force, or even appearing in the rear of the enemy, sometimes after being off-table and moved on the map.

If the Catholic guns had been better sited, so as to provide a more effective counter to the Huguenot artillery, Joyeuse might not have charged when he did, but it seems in character for the Catholic commander so impetuously to 'prove himself. Any other course would raise his 'below average' classification as a commander.

If Henry's line had a weak point, it was his left flank, where failure on the part of the Huguenot infantry might have resulted in trouble from this quarter. However, so fast did events move once the Catholics charged, it is doubtful whether a Catholic attack from this flank would have seriously affected the eventual course of the conflict.

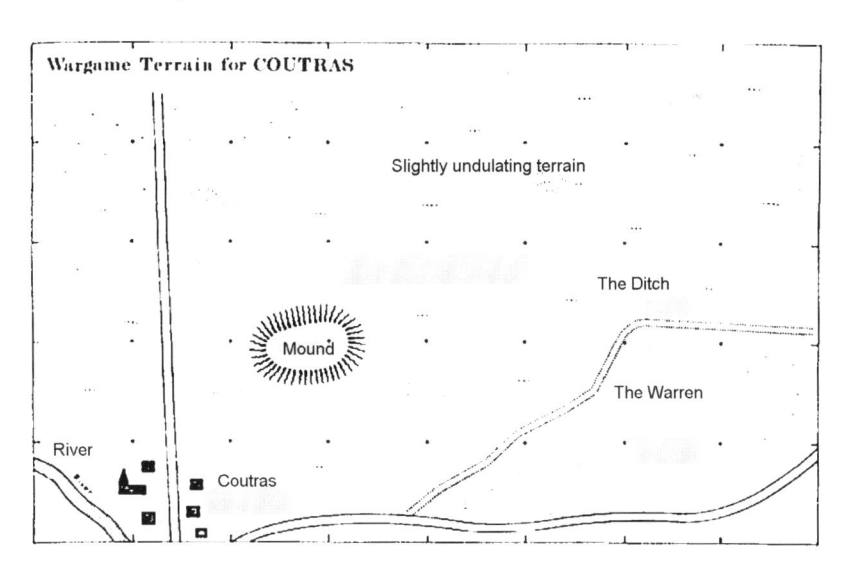

*Wargame Terrain for COUTRAS*

A tangible Military Possibility lies in what would have happened had the *enfants perdus* in the Huguenot centre fired too early, or had failed to stand in the face of the onrushing cavalry? Another concerns the Huguenot troops in the Warren, for if they had given way, Henry would have been in an unenviable position, as his exit routes were thoroughly inadequate. On the wargames table it is as unlikely that the Warren will be overrun as it was in reality, because, although the attacking infantry might have begun as first-class troops, reaching the Warren and attacking brings them 'fatigue penalties'. These, coupled with the bonuses given to defending troops positioned in a ditch, would make it unlikely that such an attack would succeed.

It is interesting finally to speculate on the course of the battle had Clermont d'Amboise not arrived at all with his artillery pieces, or arrived too late to have much effect upon the course of the battle. In these circumstances, of course, the battle might have been fought quite differently.

# 8. The Battle of Arques 21 September 1589

THE DUKE of Mayenne's Catholic army, pursuing a small Huguenot army under Henry of Navarre (now *de jure* King of France), found the defences of Dieppe too strong and decided to approach the town from the south-west by marching southwards round the estuary of the Bethune River. To do this Mayenne had to force the defile of Arques, four miles south of Dieppe and dominated by an old castle that had been modernised with artillery platforms commanding the road. It was a perfect defile, constricted by high ground around the village of Martin Eglise on one side and by the Foret d'Arques, a steep and thickly wooded hill, on the other. The road, traversing an area not more than four hundred yards wide, was bordered on one side by river marshes at its lowest point; where it was narrowest, there was a chapel, La Maladerie.

Across the defile at a point by the chapel where it was sunken and narrow, the Huguenots dug a trench and threw up an earthwork, with gaps at either end for the cavalry to sally out. The chapel, in the centre of the line, was barricaded and its parapet covered by a battery of four guns sited on a mound of earth. Five hundred yards back, where the road was sunk and bordered by a high hedge that provided cover for the arquebusiers, a second trench was dug from the edge of the marsh to the foot of the wooded hill. This trench and the area around it was commanded by the guns in the castle, but the first trench and the chapel were out of their range.

Henry had his army of about 8,000 men positioned before dawn, with the first line held by 1,200 pikes of the Royal Swiss, 600 landsknechts and about 1,200 men of five depleted regiments of French arquebusiers. The second trench was held by Galatti's Swiss Guard and the rest of the French infantry. His 1,000 cuirassed pistoleers were placed behind the first trench on each side of the high road, and there was a small cavalry reserve by the second trench.

At the head of 4,000 horse and more than 20,000 infantry, half of them Catholic-Swiss and landsknechts, Mayenne came up to the position in a long column headed by masses of horse. He sent forward Collato's landsknechts to push through the closely grown timber on the steep hillside to the right of the first trench. Two French foot regiments were to follow. The landsknechts arrived disordered and scattered at the edge of the wood, where they put their caps on their pikes, crying that they were good Protestants and would not fight their friends. Completely deceived, the occupants of the trench cheered and welcomed them, allowing the Germans to collect round that end of the defences. When a large group had assembled, the supposed deserters suddenly formed their ranks and flung themselves on the surprised and unprepared Swiss, pushing them back in disorder, so that they abandoned their position and allowed the landsknechts to push along the line, taking it and the chapel from the rear.

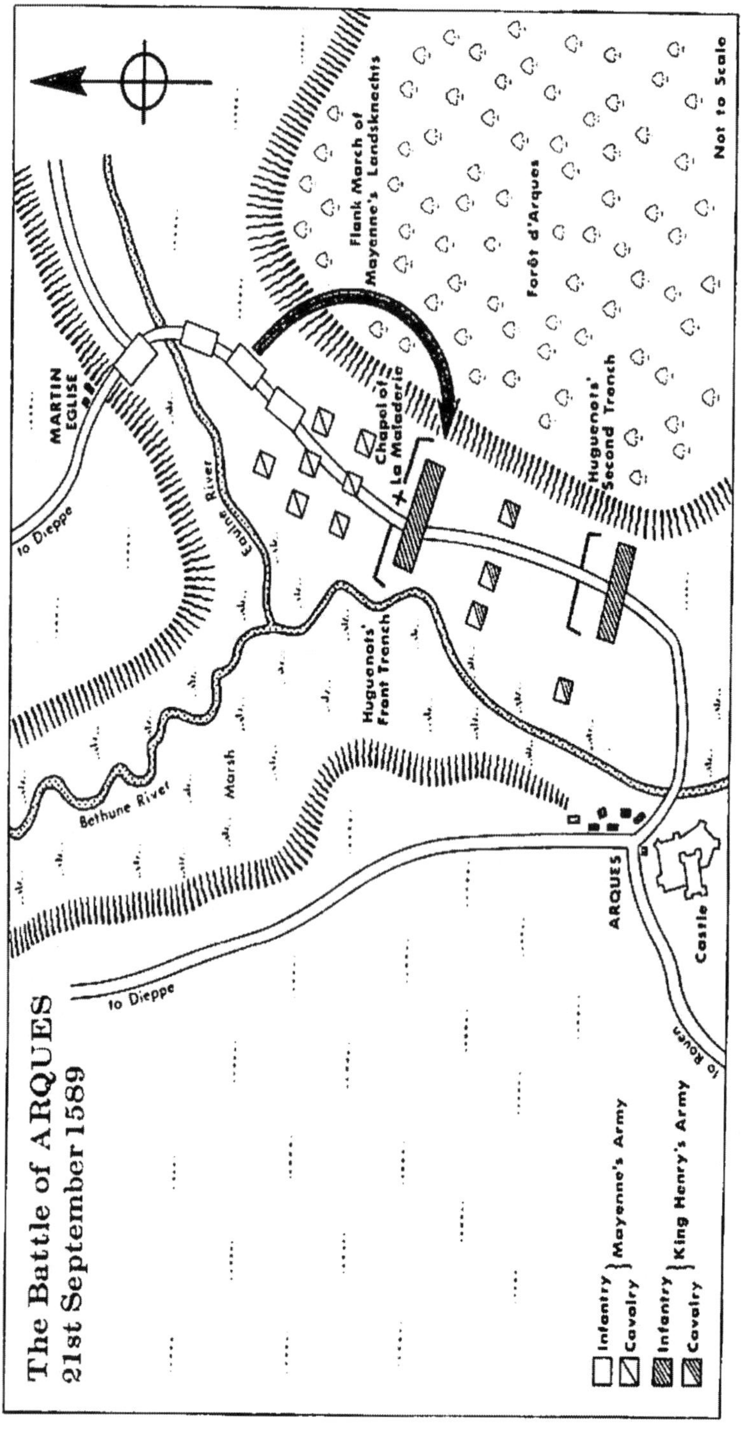
The Battle of ARQUES
21st September 1589
to Dieppe
to Dieppe
MARTIN EGLISE
Bethune River
Eaulne River
Marsh
Huguenots' Front Trench
Chapel of La Maladeria
Flank March of Mayenne's Landsknechts
Forêt d'Arques
Huguenots' Second Trench
ARQUES
Castle
to Rouen
Not to Scale
Infantry
Cavalry
Mayenne's Army
Infantry
Cavalry
King Henry's Army

In the front line at the time, Henry of Navarre was carried back by the fleeing Swiss infantry, crying out: 'Are there not fifty gentlemen of France who will come and die with their king?' This urgent appeal was answered by his horsemen charging forward at Mayenne's three squadrons of Royal Horse (800-900 men), who were pouring through the gaps at the ends of the line. Although there were only about 150 of them, the Huguenot cavalry charged and counter-charged to drive the Catholic horseback beyond the chapel in a sprawling mêlée that lasted for an hour. Then the arrival of four more of Mayenne's squadrons pushed the Huguenots slowly back until they were able to rally on some 150 of their own cavalry under the Count Auvergne. Together they went forward again, driving the enemy before them to the turn of the road, when they could see a huge mass of some 3,000 Catholic horse, who pushed them back past the abandoned first trench and the chapel until halted by flanking fire from Huguenot arquebusiers lining the hedgerows of the sunken road.

While all this was going on, attempts by Huguenot infantry to storm the first trench had been beaten off by the landsknechts, and now both Huguenot cavalry and infantry had to retire to the second trench. Here the Swiss Guard had remained firm and their pikes, backed by the fire of flanking arquebusiers lining the hedgerows, brought the Catholics to a complete standstill. Mayenne's men were so tightly packed as to make manoeuvre impossible, and he tried to break the deadlock by turning Henry's left with 500 horsemen sent through the marsh; but their chargers sank to their bellies in the mud, so that their riders had to abandon them and struggle out on foot. Pistols empty and swords blunted, Henry's cavalry managed to rally and again went forward, only to see Mayenne's entire force stretching back along the road, rolling towards them.

The end of the unequal struggle seemed to be nigh when the fog that had been lying low over the battlefield throughout the morning suddenly lifted to reveal a perfect massed target to the impatient gunners standing on the parapet of the castle of Arques. At once they opened fire on the tightly packed ranks of the approaching Catholics, their shot causing lanes and gaps to appear in their column, so that they were forced back out of artillery range round the bend in the road. Seeing themselves left behind by their cavalry, the landsknechts occupying the first trench put up a poor resistance as Henry advanced with his Swiss, both the rallied and the reserve, in a column flanked with arquebusiers, to storm the chapel and earthworks and send the German mercenaries fleeing back up the road.

Henry's Huguenots halted and occupied their original position as the enemy withdrew. The Catholics had employed only a third of their infantry and half of their cavalry, whereas Henry had used every man in his army. The casualties were not very heavy, Mayenne losing 600 men against the 200 of the Huguenots. So ended the extraordinary Battle of Arques, certainly one of the most notable recorded cases of the defence of a defile where superior numbers were useless if they could not be deployed.

### Reconstructing the Battle as a Wargame

Set up the table with the Huguenots in position. Mayenne's force appears on the table at the start of game-move No 1 in his historical order of battle. Provided Mayenne's onslaughts follow in correct historical sequence, the wargame will fight itself out in a reasonably realistic fashion.

The ruse that allowed the landsknechts to take the first Huguenot line of defence can be simulated by accepting it as a fact, by placing the German mercenaries near the right-hand end of the defences (in some disarray and disorder as they have just emerged from the heavily wooded area), and then forming them up and sending them in to the attack. The Swiss will take a part of that move to assess the situation before responding to the landsknechts' move. The battle can follow a reasonably realistic course if the Swiss take a proportion (a third or a half) of the game-move to assess the situation, and then, outnumbered, mêlée at a disadvantage so that the eventual result will probably be authentic. 'Weighted' Chance Cards can be used to control the landsknechts' actions, though there is a risk of the landsknechts' ploy not working.

The fog lifting near the end of the battle can be simulated by merely accepting that it happened. If it is desired that there be some doubt as to whether the fog really did lift (although this is a departure from historical reality), two decimal dice can be thrown, allowing a 90 per cent chance of the fog lifting and a 10 per cent chance of it lying low over the field, to prevent the artillery in the Castle of Arques from opening fire.

### Classification of Commanders

Henry of Navarre, the Huguenot leader, displayed a sense of tactics that must classify him as an 'above average' commander. The Duke of Mayenne displayed a reasonably intelligent approach by first sending in his landsknechts to outflank the position rather than the cavalry in a bull-at-a-gate charge. The manner in which the battle unfolded after the initial success of the landsknechts more or less controlled the Catholic leader's subsequent tactics. Without really doing anything wrong, Mayenne, by comparison with Henry of Navarre on this occasion, must rank as an 'average' commander.

These comparative ratings should be considered in the light of their balancing effect upon the course of the table-top battle between forces with a considerable numerical disparity.

### Quality of Troops

The factors that control the running of an enjoyable wargame in a situation where one side is much stronger than the other fall under three headings:
1 The comparative quality of the troops on both sides, with the smaller force ideally being superior.
2 The state of morale of the two sides, both initially and during the stress of combat — this factor is considered at length under **Morale**.

3 The terrain, whose nature must present the smaller side with undoubted tactical advantages —also considered at greater length under **Terrain**.

Every Huguenot unit or formation displayed enough courage and stamina to rank as 'elite' -even the Swiss infantry in the first trench, who were forced out of their position through their gullibility rather than any lack of courage, and later in the battle atoned for their early error. The vastly outnumbered Huguenot cavalry displayed fighting qualities of a consistently high nature in the face of great odds. The Catholic cavalry, although some 8-900 against 150 Huguenots, were consistently pushed back in a mêlée that is said to have lasted an hour. Ordinarily such inability to defeat an inferior force would lead us to classify the Catholics as second-class troops, but the nature of the terrain caused the cavalry mêlée to be fought on a limited frontage, so that the numerical disparity of the Catholic cavalry was nullified. It may therefore be classed as 'average', like the remainder of the Catholic army.

**Morale**
The essential balancing effect of giving the smaller force a higher morale classification when it is taking on a larger one allows the Huguenots to hold on in the face of great odds, and eventually win. The Huguenot cavalry must certainly be given such a bonus, or else, when the retreating Swiss pour past them after being dislodged from the first trench, the bad fortune of a poor dice throw may result in the low morale rating that may cause them to break.

At the end of the battle the landsknechts in the first trench put up a very poor resistance when they saw that they had been abandoned. In much the same way Mayenne's troops in the vicinity of the second trench did not display much stomach when the artillery opened up on them from the Castle of Arques. If these two situations are to be authentically simulated, it might be advantageous to 'weigh' the morale effects (by doubling dice deductions, for example) at this stage of the battle.

**Effect and Construction of Terrain**
The importance of the defile of Arques lay in the fact that it presented only a very narrow fighting frontage, so forcing the numerically superior Catholics to attack with no more troops than their enemy had to oppose them. All important, this factor completely controlled the course of the battle by ensuring, for example, that the Huguenot cavalry (outnumbered five or six to one) were not only able to hold on but also to get the better of their mêlée with the Catholic horsemen.
This terrain should be constructed lengthways along the table with the defile bordered on both sides by rising ground, heavily timbered on one flank and with an uncrossable river and impassable marsh on the other. Although its narrowness will inevitably bring about a jumbled

# Wargame Terrain for ARQUES

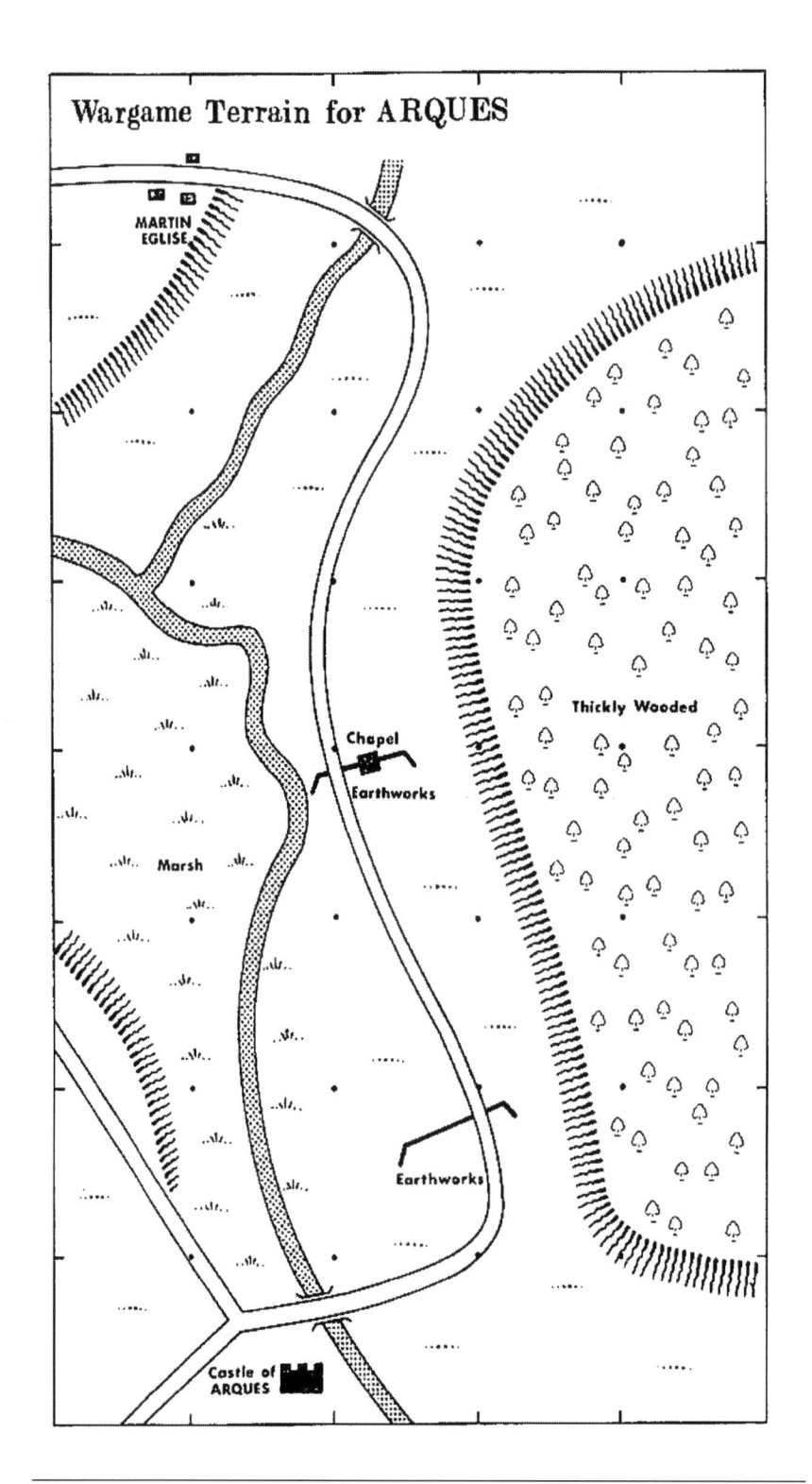

MARTIN EGLISE

Chapel
Earthworks

Marsh

Thickly Wooded

Earthworks

Castle of ARQUES

mêlée-ridden wargame, the temptation to widen the defile, and nullify the beneficial effects that this terrain gives to the numerically inferior force, should be resisted.

**Military Possibilities**
Had the Swiss refused to be fooled by the landsknechts' protestations of peace, undoubtedly the German mercenaries, in scattered disarray and disorder after toiling through the heavily timbered hillside, would have been turned back. In this case it is unlikely that the attackers would ever have penetrated further than the first line of defence — and the battle would have lost any pretence of similarity with reality.

If the landsknechts, after taking the first trench, had turned the abandoned Huguenot battery of four guns on to the subsequent counterattacks by their late owners, it is extremely unlikely that the Huguenots would ever have recaptured the position. Perhaps the landsknechts did in fact use the guns in this manner, although, under the stress of battle, it might have proved too difficult completely to turn the four guns, whose wheels were probably well sunk into the mound of earth on which they were sited. If these guns had fired, their recoil would have 'dug them in', so as to make it impossible to turn them.

Had the outflanking Catholic cavalry managed to force its way through the marsh during the second stage of the battle, Henry's position would have been rendered untenable. But the undoubted value of the marsh as an obstacle was a prime reason for Henry selecting this defensive position in the first place.

# 9. The Battle of Nieuport 2 July 1600

THIS, THE most brilliant victory achieved by Prince Maurice of Orange during his long military career, was a most interesting fight from a tactical point of view. Maurice intended to besiege Nieuport, and numerous Dutch ships bearing provisions and munitions from Ostend, having sailed in conjunction with his army, were moored in the tidal estuary of the Yser River. A recent mutiny in the Spanish Low Country forces had led the Dutch to believe that they would be uninterrupted, so that Maurice was surprised when he received the news that the Austrian Archduke Albert, ruler of the Spanish Netherlands (Belgium today), was close at hand with a field army of unknown strength, having recaptured numerous recently taken small fortresses and positions. By thrusting himself between Maurice and his base at Ostend, and with a fortified town behind him, the Archduke had forced the Dutch leader either to accept battle or embark his army, probably losing at least his rearguard in the process.

The Archduke had been able to raise an army because the Spanish soldiers, although in a state of mutiny, were proud of their military reputation and hated the thought of the Spanish Netherlands falling into Dutch hands. They responded, therefore, to the Archduke's desperate appeal to their religious fanaticism and esprit de corps, and agreed to join him, provided they served under their own standards and chosen officers, with an honourable place in the vanguard during the battle.

On hearing of the Spaniards' approach, Maurice sent Ernest of Nassau with Edmond's Scottish Regiment of Foot, Van der Noot's Zealand Foot Regiment. 400 horse and 2 field pieces, to delay the Spaniards by seizing the important bridge at Leffinghem, unaware that the Archduke had already captured it. Coming upon the enemy in force, Ernest was almost cut to pieces, only two fugitives arriving back at Nieuport to reveal the disaster.

At 8am on 2 July, when the water was low enough to uncover the fords, Maurice pushed his 'vaward', under Francis Vere, across the river, to deploy on the broad dry beach and cover the passage of the rest of the army, as the incoming tide made it essential for them to have plenty of time to cross and form battle order. The 'vaward', far stronger than the 'main-battle' or the 'rearward', consisted of 41 companies of foot — 4,000 of the best infantry in the army, made up of the Veres' 2 foot regiments (Francis with 13 companies and Horace with 11), a strong Frisian regiment of 17 companies under Colonel Hertinga, and 2 companies of Maurice's own Foot Guards —and more than half the Dutch cavalry force (9 units out of the 17), mostly picked troops under Count Louis of Nassau, Lieutenant-General of the Horse, and including cuirassiers and 3 cornets (or troops) of light horse. The cavalry led the advance, with the light horse well forward in a scouting role. The 'vaward's' 6 field guns, served by sailors, were planted on the

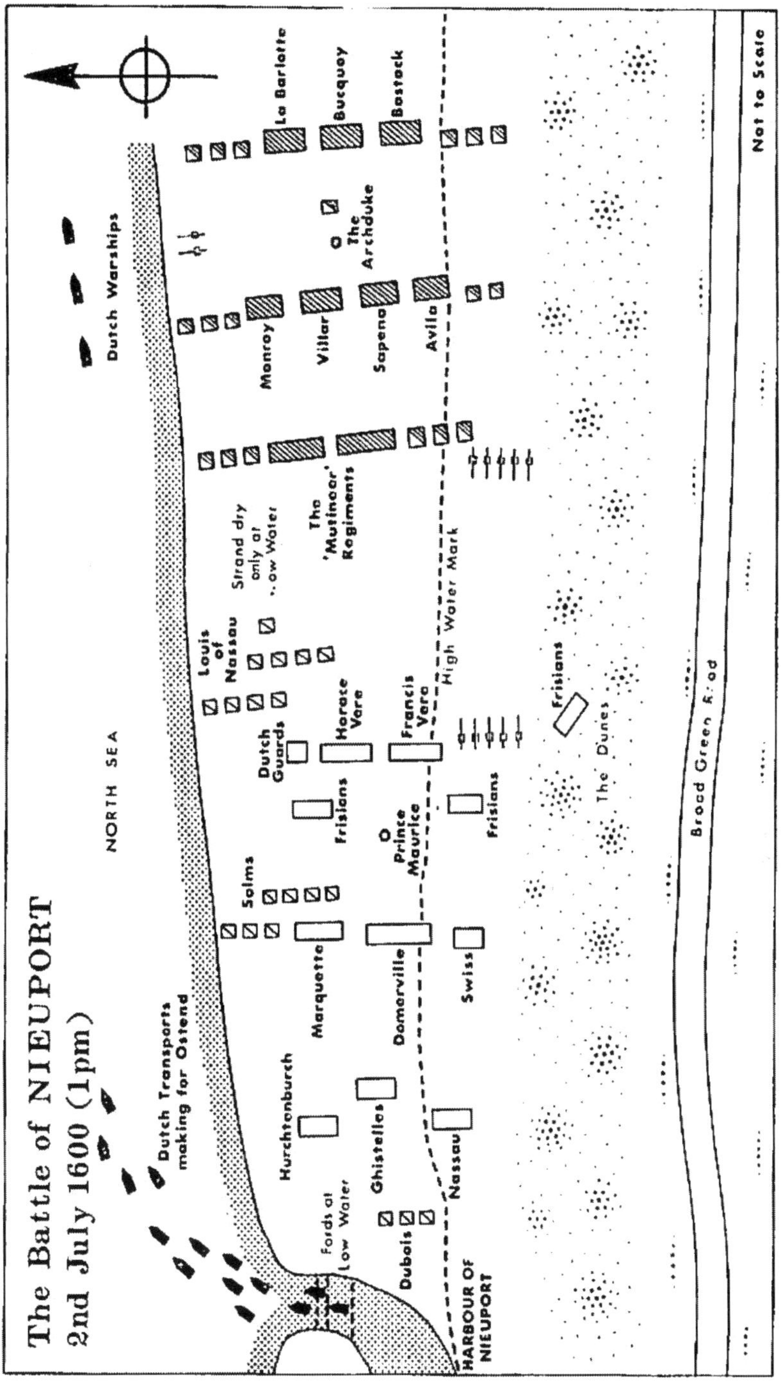
The Battle of NIEUPORT
2nd July 1600 (1pm)
Dutch Transports making for Ostend
Dutch Warships
NORTH SEA
Fords at Low Water
HARBOUR OF NIEUPORT
Dubois
Ghistelles
Hurchtenburch
Nassau
Marquette
Domerville
Swiss
Solms
Prince Maurice
Frisians
Dutch Guards
Horace Vere
Francis Vere
Frisians
Louis of Nassau
Strand dry only at Low Water
The 'Mutineer' Regiments
High Water Mark
Frisians
The Dunes
Broad Green Road
Monroy
Villar
Sapena
Avila
The Archduke
La Barlotte
Bucquoy
Bostock
Not to Scale

dry sand at the foot of the Dunes, with 6 companies of Frisians in support.

The 'main-battle' followed, and much later the 'rearward', which had remained before Nieuport in case the garrison was tempted to sally out and destroy the ships stranded on the mudflats. This force was still crossing the estuary when cavalry skirmishes opened the battle. Maurice's total strength, after deducting the losses at Leffinghem, was 10,000 infantry, 1,500 cavalry and 7 guns. As his forces arrived on the east side of the estuary, Maurice drew them up on the firm beach left uncovered by the low tide. It was broad enough for the whole army to be drawn up on it, but at high tide it shrunk to between fifty and one hundred yards of firm sand leading up to the Dunes — undulating sandhills between 350 and 700 yardds wide, whose loose sand was overgrown with furze bushes and other low scrub. The country road from Ostend, a broad green track, ran on the far side of the Dunes.

It was anticipated that the Spanish would advance on this road, but soon it became evident that they were coming along the beach. Their army consisted of about 90 companies of foot (10,000 men); about 1,500 horsemen, comprising 6 cornets of pistoleers (cuirassiers), 4 of *herrueleros* (light horse) and 9 much smaller cornets of 'lances' or men-at-arms; and 6 demi-cannons and 2 smaller pieces. The 'mutineers', an assorted collection of Spaniards and Walloons, were an unruly but formidable body of men formed in 2 provisional foot regiments and a cavalry force of 600 horse, all under Francisco de Mendoza and forming the Spanish 'vaward'. Next came the Archduke with the 'main-battle' containing the 'flower of the army' — 3 old Spanish tercios, commanded by Alonzo di Avila, Louis de Villar and Jernnimo Monroy respectively, and 1 old Italian tercio under Gasparo Sapena. The Archduke had one cornet of the lancers of his guard as escort and 5 more were attached to the 'main-battle'. The two Walloon regiments of La Barlotte and Bucquoy, with Bostock's Irish regiment and 6 cornets of horse, formed the 'rearward'.

The first Spaniards to appear were 10 cornets of cavalry, which took up the whole area between the sandhills and the sea, and soon there was some cavalry bickering between the Dutch light horse and the Spanish *herrueleros.* Then Francis Vere ordered Count Louis to fall his horse in on the left of the deployed infantry close to the water's edge as the Dutch skirmishers slowly gave way in front, harassed by cornets of the 'mutineer' cavalry, who swerved off in disorder when they came under the fire of the Dutch guns higher up the beach.

The fires of battle flickered and died when the Archduke realised that the beach was rapidly narrowing as the tide came in. Several Dutch warships lying off the coast began to send long shots into the flank of the Spanish army, causing the Archduke to order two guns to be brought to the water's edge to reply to their fire. But the tide was coming in fast and more Dutch warships were appearing, so at 2.30 the Spaniards began laboriously to march off the beach up on to the soft shifting sands of the Dunes. It was an operation that took nearly two hours, until only five guns and some infantry companies remained on the beach facing the Dutch battery. The Spanish cavalry, except for one cornet, crossed the Dunes and formed up on the broad green road, while their infantry slowly trudged westward, keeping their formations with difficulty on the deep uneven sandhills.

The Spanish move off the beach was largely dictated by the incoming tide plus the flanking fire from the Dutch warships, but the Archduke may also have been aware of the inferiority of his cavalry, who were consistently ridden down by the Dutch cuirassiers, and decided to trust the battle to his strong veteran infantry units, which might gain the upper hand in the sand dunes. The Archduke was not unjustified in this assumption, as Maurice's motley infantry consisted of 2 English, 1 French, 1 Walloon, 1 German, 1 Swiss and only 3 native Dutch corps.

With plenty of time to manoeuvre, the Dutch deployed to conform to the Spanish dispositions. Leaving 5 Frisian and 2 English companies to protect the guns, with 3 cornets of horse from the 'main-battle' in reserve, Vere sent the rest of his infantry up to join the 6 companies of Frisians already on the Dunes, arranging them behind a low sandhill, with 250 picked English infantry and Dutch Foot Guards as a 'Forlorn Hope' on a high isolated flat-topped sandhill projecting to his left front. The sailors dragged two guns from the battery on the shore on to a still higher sandhill to their right, so commanding the green road below them and on their right. On lower ground in front of these guns Vere placed 500 Frisian musketeers, whose range of fire also included any enemy approaching by the road. The rest of the English and Dutch infantry were drawn up in small supporting detachments ready to reinforce the front line. Count Louis's cavalry had gone about, to pass laboriously across the sandhills, where they continued the line of infantry by drawing up on the green road. The 'main-battle' and the 'rearward' came up and were placed behind Vere's line, with the infantry mainly on the southern side of the dunes and the cavalry supporting the 'vaward' horsemen on the green road.

The 'main-battle' consisted of the strong Huguenot/French regiment of Domerville in the centre, flanked on the right by a small Swiss battalion of 400 men and on the left by Marquette's Walloon regiment. Composed entirely of deserters from the Spanish colours, the Walloons were the only doubtful element in the Dutch army, but they fought well, probably because they knew that death would be the penalty for defeat. There was not a single Dutchman among the infantry of the 'main-battle'. Also in the force were 6 cornets of Dutch cavalry commanded by Count Solms, and 2 cornets of English cavalry under Sir Edward Cecil and Captain Pembroke. The 'rearward' consisted of the German regiment of Ernest of Nassau, commanded by Lt-Col Huysmann; the 2 Dutch regiments of Hurchtenburch and Ghistelles, the latter less 6 of its companies, which had been left in the defences outside Ostend; and 2 cornets of Dutch and 1 of English horse under Dubois.

Advancing slowly through the shifting sands of the Dunes, the Spanish infantry in three lines neared the Dutch position, and 500 arquebusiers of the 'mutineer' regiments went forward to attack Vere's 'Forlorn Hope' on the advance sandhill. They were beaten back, as were some 500 pikemen and arquebusiers drawn from the regiments behind the mutineers. Now replacing the exhausted mutineers with the three Spanish and the Italian tercios, the Archduke made a general advance against the whole of Vere's front, with Monroy's and Villar's tercios attacking the left of the Dutch line, while Avila's and Sapena's attacked south of the two-gun battery on the high sandhill. Maurice brought up from his 'main-battle' Domerville's Huguenot regiment and the Swiss and Walloons to support his right, but sent no aid to Vere on the northern flank, although it was repeatedly requested. It might be claimed that Prince Maurice was able to keep his third line of infantry still intact when the Archduke's 'rearward' reserve had been committed by sacrificing Vere's English and Frisian 'vaward', which not only took on the Spanish 'vaward' the 'mutineers' — but at least two of the four tercios of the Spanish 'main-battle', without receiving a single reinforcement.

While the infantry attacks and counterattacks were proceeding on the undulating surface of the Dunes, the Spanish cavalry, advancing on the low ground inland, were completely routed by Louis's force, aided by crossfire from the two guns on the sandhill and by Vere's Frisian musketeers. Hotly pursued, the disordered cavalry fell back to shelter behind the infantry of its own 'rearward', though many scattered and left the battlefield; it is recorded that the 'mutineer' horse showed up very badly. In this action Louis was only rescued from capture by a desperate cavalry charge, and it took a long time for him to re-order his squadrons and charge again on the Spanish left flank across the green road, to drive in the cavalry of the Archduke's 'main-battle'. Then Louis's depleted and exhausted squadrons were checked by crossfire from the Spanish 'rearward' infantry.

The Archduke threw in his third line, the Walloon and Irish regiments of Bucquoy, La Barlotte and Bostock, in a thrust against Vere's unreinforced section of the Dutch front line, where all the reserves had been used up. The English and Frisian infantry companies were driven off the dunes in disorder, slowly pursued by the exhausted Spanish infantry, who were mixed up in a hopeless confusion of pikemen and musketeers, so that they dissolved like the mob they were when attacked by cavalry. The retreating Dutch infantry fell back behind the battery on the shore, where a few hundred of them rallied while the guns kept up their fire on the opposing Spanish battery, although almost out of ammunition. Then Maurice threw in his reserve cavalry — the cornets of Pembroke, Balen and Sir Edward Cecil -- to charge headlong into the mass of disordered Spanish infantry, and send them flying in all directions among the dunes.

Seeing their confusion, Vere's infantry rallied and pressed forward against little opposition, Count Louis's weary cavalry charged once more on the green road, and Maurice ordered his 'rearward' regiments on the dunes to make a general advance. Suddenly enemy resistance collapsed, as the thoroughly demoralised Spanish cavalry, fleeing past their flank, caused the infantry on the dunes to break up and retire in a disorderly mass of pikemen and musketeers towards the Leffinghem bridge, their natural line of retreat. Reinvigorated, the Dutch cavalry rode them down on all sides, destroying nearly half the Archduke's weary infantry, which were slaughtered wholesale, losing about 3,000 men. The four 'old' tercios and the 'mutineers' were almost wiped out, and the Dutch captured 105 out of 120 standards of horse and foot on the field. The cavalry escaped more lightly, but the majority of the Spanish leaders, including the Archduke himself, were wounded, and some were killed or captured. The Dutch lost about 2,000, including the casualties at Leffinghem bridge. The two English regiments in the 'vaward' lost 600 men out of their 24 companies.

Nieuport was a battle where the stubborness and endurance of the Dutch and English infantry enabled them to stand long enough for their tired cavalry to make the final attack against the similarly exhausted Spaniards. In the arduous conditions amid the sandhills the Archduke failed to understand that by dusk his infantry, which had been under arms for twelve hours, was exhausted. Throughout military history it is a notable fact that mounted commanders and staff officers habitually failed to notice the fatigue of their infantry.

The echoes of the earlier debacle at Leffinghem Bridge were still resounding when the battle ended. If Prince Maurice had not sent out the small force that was destroyed at Leffinghem earlier in the day, the Dutch army, 2,500 men stronger, would probably have seen off the Spaniards even more easily. In addition, if the Dutch garrison at Ostend had sallied out and seized Leffinghem bridge, the whole of the Spanish army would have been captured; their hesitation was perhaps due to their awareness of the disaster of the morning, when the Scottish and Zealand regiments had been wiped out.

**Reconstructing the Battle as a Wargame**
This battle can be reconstructed as a wargame in two distinctly different styles, both of them having an authentic bearing on what in fact happened, but with differing tactical aspects. The first sees the Dutch crossing the river and attempting to take up their battle order on the flat beach in the face of Spanish attempts to destroy them piecemeal before their assembly is complete. In fact, the Dutch 'rearward' was still crossing the river when the cavalry skirmish opened the battle, so that even a small increase in the speed of the Spanish approach might well have caught the Dutch before they were fully disposed. In these circumstances both sides will initially skirmish and then join battle, until the tide forces everyone slowly inland on to the Dunes. The guns of the 'off-table' Dutch fleet will no doubt play an important role in discouraging the Spanish approach.

Refighting the battle in this manner makes it essential that both forces follow a strict order of march, ensuring that those units that formed the historical 'vaward' come first on to the field, followed by the 'main-battle' and then the 'rearward' — all composed of the forces that made up these formations in 1600.

The second style presents a more authentic and straightforward wargame by staging the battle as it occurred amid the shifting sands of the undulating Dunes, by initially setting out both sides as at the start of the battle in their historical dispositions. The 'scenario' controlling the battle will chart the order of attacks and an approximation of the moves in which they take place.

As at Pinkie, the warships are 'off-table', positioned so that their gunfire just reaches the beach.

**Classification of Commanders**
Prince Maurice of Nassau consistently displayed a high quality of generalship throughout his military career, and it is generally accepted that at Nieuport he reached his peak. He must obviously be classified as an 'above average' commander. Some Great Captains of military history have earned their titles because they had the good fortune to encounter enemy commanders of poor capability. The Archduke Albert was a reasonably good commander, however, since he managed to collect an army although many of his troops were in a state of mutiny, and by moving fast secured such key posts as the bridge at Leffinghem and recaptured sundry castles and other positions. Believing in the quality of his troops, he endeavoured to provide them with a suitable battleground by attempting to fight on the level beach, but it must count against him that he misjudged the state of the tide, and failed to realise that the unopposed Dutch ships lying close offshore would fire on him. All these things considered, however, the Archduke Albert does not deserve to be rated lower than 'average', and a trifle unfortunate to find himself facing such an enemy commander as Prince Maurice of Nassau.

**Quality of Troops and Morale**
The following Dutch formations are entitled to be ranked as 'elite' troops and to be given the usual benefits of bonus points when assessing fighting ability and morale: the Dutch cavalry, Vere's infantry, the Dutch Foot Guards, and the Frisian infantry.

The other units on each side were good solid average troops, none deserving to be ranked as 'below average' — not even the Spanish cavalry. Light horse such as the *herrueleros* were invariably crushed by the Dutch cuirassiers, but even the most unorthodox wargames rules usually allow 'elite' heavy cavalry to defeat 'average' light horse.

It is stressed in reports of this battle that the performance of the Spanish troops was greatly affected by fatigue, as was to be expected after they had trudged up and down steep sand dunes in heavy boots and uniform, carrying full kit, equipment and a weighty musket or pike. To carry out such heavy physical effort during the stress and anxiety of battle must inevitably exact a heavy toll. A method of simulating the cumulative effects of fatigue is described in the Coutras reconstruction, and it is suggested that this be applied to the Spanish troops at the Battle of Nieuport.

All troops on both sides began the battle in a first-class state of morale, which remained steady or fell during the course of the battle.

**Effects and Construction of Terrain**
Although it is quite likely that Prince Maurice's allied army would have won this battle in any circumstances, there is no doubt that the ground over which the Battle of Nieuport was fought played an important part in the conflict. The incoming tide caused both sides to redeploy, which, coupled with the march to the field and then through the dunes, tired both Spanish and Dutch troops, but more the former, because they had marched further.

The undulations of the sand dunes limited vision, so that a formation knew little of what was happening to comrades on either flank, and Dutch possession of two of the highest mounds in the dunes must have stood them in good stead. The course of the battle indicates that the 'Forlorn Hope' on one of these elevations more than held its own, while the guns on the other played a big part in foiling the Spanish cavalry on the green road below.

Of the two different ways in which this battle can be refought, the first requires a terrain that includes the beach, the sand dunes, the green track and its surrounding flat ground, whereas the second omits the beach. Ideally this wargame should be fought on a sand table, but few wargamers possess them. The next best alternative is to strew graded shapes across the table top and drape a green cloth over them so as to produce an irregular undulating surface; these varying gradients should not be too steep or too small to limit the practical manoeuvring of figures on their surface.

**Military Possibilities**
The forces were nearly equal in numbers, and had Maurice not lost 2,500 men at Leffinghem before the battle, his force, which was already of superior quality, would have won the battle more easily.

Archduke Albert might have judged the tide better and been able to continue his advance on the beach, so making contact before the Dutch 'rearward' was over the river. It could then have been awkward for the Dutch, but the Spanish advantage might well have been neutralised by flanking fire from the Dutch warships.

Had Prince Maurice reinforced Vere when requested, the 'vaward' would not have finally retreated. But then the exhausted and completely disarrayed Spanish infantry would not have pursued, to leave themselves open to the cavalry attack that brought about their eventual destruction.

If Maurice had reinforced Vere, the diminished numbers at the point from which the reinforcements were taken might have suffered during subsequent fighting, and as Maurice ended the battle with his third line intact, it seems highly likely that the reinforcements would have been taken from that source.

# Wargame Terrain for NIEUPORT

Flat Ground

The Broad Green Road

Hill for Sailors' Guns

Mound for 'Forlorn Hope'

Undulating Sand Dunes
(dotted with furze bushes and low scrub)

Beach & Sea

# 10. The Battle of Breitenfeld 18 September 1631

BY 1631 the Thirty Years War, which had been devastating Europe for thirteen years, entered its third phase — the Swedish period. Opposing Gustavus Adolphus, King of Sweden, was the Imperial army commanded by the seventy-two year old General Count Johan Tilly ('The Monk in Armour'), a veteran Walloon who had learned his trade under Parma, trailing a pike in a Spanish tercio in the Netherlands. He was a good commander in the conventional Spanish tradition.

In the summer of 1631 Tilly, after laying waste the surrounding countryside, marched into unravaged Saxony, where the excesses of his army drove John George I, Elector of Saxony, to join forces with the Swedish army. The combined force of 26,000 Swedes and 16,000 Saxons hurried southward across the Elbe to intercept Tilly. The opposing armies met at Breitenfeld, six miles north of Leipzig, where, on a dusty, slightly undulating plain, bare of trees but crossed by a marshy stream, a precipitate action by Tilly's second-in-command, Count Pappenheim, committed him to battle.

On a bright, hot September morning Tilly drew up his army on a two-mile front. His 35,000 infantry were positioned in two lines of tercios— 17 solid squares each of 1,500 men, 50 men deep —and his cavalry stationed on either flank, the left wing comprising 5,000 Black Cuirassiers under Pappenheim, and the right 5,000 horsemen under Furstenberg and Isolani. His light guns were placed in front of the Imperial centre and his heavy guns between the centre and the right — 26 pieces of artillery in all. The Imperial army had the advantage of position on a gentle downward slope, with sun and wind at its back.

Tilly had an excellent view as Gustavus Adolphus drew up his army some 1,500 yards away in a formation that looked more and more like a chessboard as the Swedish infantry brigades and cavalry regiments took up their positions. On the far left the Saxon infantry formed a solid block, with cavalry on either flank. Next to them came the Swedish left under Horn, comprising 3 regiments of cavalry interspersed with detachments of musketeers, backed by 2 more cavalry regiments in the second line. Gustavus himself commanded the centre, whose front line was made up of 4 brigades of foot in their characteristic T-shaped formation; a second line of 2 brigades of infantry and 1 cavalry regiment, and a third line of 3 brigades of foot supported by 2 regiments of cavalry. The Swedish right comprised 6 cavalry regiments interspersed with musketeers in the first line, 1 cavalry regiment behind them, and 4 more forming a third line. Every regiment had its two regimental 4-pounder guns to its front, and Torstensson's heavier field artillery was massed in front of the centre. In all there were 100 guns — 60 Swedish and 40 Saxon.

Some reports say that Tilly began the battle by sending out 2,000 cavalry as skirmishers, to be hotly engaged and driven back by Swedish dragoons supported by Scots mercenaries. It seems quite feasible that this happened before the Swedish army, in its battle formation, advanced across the marshy stream at noon and began a cannonade that persisted for two hours. The numerically superior and faster-firing Swedish guns had much the best of the exchange. Eventually, galled beyond endurance by the heavy fire that was ploughing through their tightly packed ranks, the Imperialist cavalry, without orders from Tilly, spurred forward — on the right Furstenberg's Croat horsemen, and on the left the fiery Pappenheim's Black Cuirassiers.

In an avalanche of crimson cloaks and gleaming blades the Croats fell upon the 16,000 inexperienced Saxon soldiers, causing them to waver and then flee from the field in a blind rout, encouraged by their own guns turned on them by the Imperialists. But a far sterner reception met the Black Cuirassiers as they swung out leftwards to thunder down upon the Swedish flank. Gustavus countered by swinging the 5 supporting cavalry regiments of Baner's wing to form a new flank at right-angles to the front line in a V-shaped defensive salient. Pappenheim, the scarred veteran of a hundred charges, led his Black Cuirassiers forward at a fast trot no less than seven times, to discharge their wheel-lock pistols into the new Swedish flank, and each time the Imperialist horse were driven back, first being flayed by the Swedish regimental guns, and then by the muskets of the Swedish infantry. The latter would run out from between the Swedish squadrons, deploy in a well-drilled manner, with front ranks kneeling to achieve full fire-effect, then fire and return to reload while their cavalry was counterattacking. As the shaken cuirassiers fell back each time, the Swedish horsemen withdrew to the protection of their cannon and musketeers. The devastating discipline and precision of all three arms fighting together caused the Black Cuirassiers steadily to disintegrate. As their seventh charge was turned back, Baner let his horsemen go at a good round gallop instead of a trot, and the heavy Swedish cavalry, hitting the shaken horsemen at the gallop, immediately shattered and drove them from the field.

Against the Swedish left, where the Saxons' defection had left Horn's flank exposed, Tilly marched his centre infantry blocks while his right-wing tercios marched obliquely towards the open flank and rear. It was a massive manoeuvre easily countered by the mobile Swedes, whose flexibility allowed their musketeers and horsemen to change front and face the onslaught as, ordering Horn to wheel his men left, Gustavus brought across two brigades of infantry from the second line of his centre. Now followed the hardest phase of the fighting, with the outcome of the battle hanging upon it. Helmetless and wearing only a buff coat for protection, Gustavus galloped up and down the line, shouting encouragement and swinging his reddened sabre in every mêlée. Torstensson's guns tore great lanes in the mass of Imperialist foot, and the Swedish infantry brigades fired ceaseless volleys of musketry before their pike formations lurched forward to clash with the Imperialist pikemen. The Saxon guns were recaptured and turned to

# The Battle of BREITENFELD
## 18th September 1631

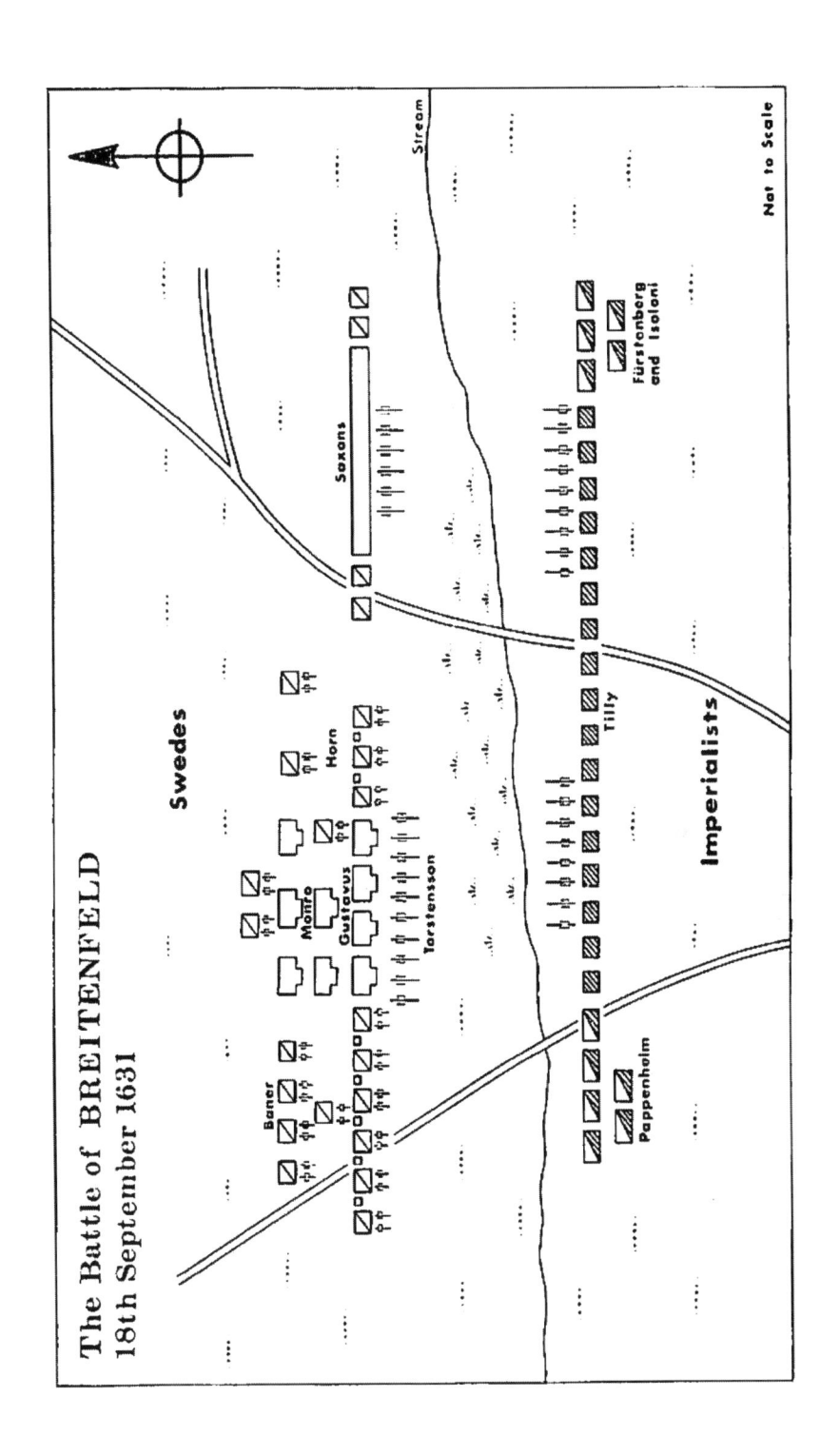

enfilade the Imperialist flank, their hail of shot causing the vast squares to waver.

Then Gustavus led four cavalry regiments from his right wing in a great charge up the slope at the enemy artillery, sweeping through the guns and round to the left to separate the Imperialist infantry from their cavalry. Assailed to the front and left simultaneously by infantry, artillery and horsemen, with their own guns turned on them and cut off from their cavalry, the close-packed masses of Imperial infantry began to melt away, and, as dusk fell over the smoke-enshrouded field, they broke and fled, the Swedish cavalry riding down the milling fugitives.

Tilly left 13,000 men dead on the field, and 7,000 men and all his artillery were captured. The captives later took service with the Swedes. Tilly himself was wounded in the neck, chest and right arm, and only a hard-fighting rearguard action by the remains of Pappenheim's Black Cuirassiers prevented an even greater disaster. The total losses of the combined Swedish-Saxon army were about 3,000, less than a third being Swedish.

**Reconstructing the Battle as a Wargame**
The Swedish victory at Breitenfeld was secured by cavalry, artillery, pikemen and musketeers mutually supporting each other in small self-contained combat groups, while their regimental guns fired three times as fast as the enemy artillery. The Swedish method of fighting was revolutionary for its day. so that attempts to reconstruct this battle (and Lutzen) should not be undertaken before studying it carefully.

Although the large Saxon force on the Swedish left flank was chased from the field in the first phase of the battle, giving the Imperialists a numerical superiority of seven to four, Gustavus Adolphus won decisively, and it is difficult to see the battle ending in any other way.

The following factors explain the reasons for Swedish superiority:
1 All branches of the Swedish army moved faster than their counterparts in the Imperialist army.
2 The Swedish musketeers, regimental guns and Torstensson's heavier guns all fired incomparably faster and more accurately than those of Tilly's army. The Swedish army had nearly four times as many guns as the Imperialists, although a large proportion of them were light 4-pounder mobile regimental guns.
3 The Swedish method of cavalry fighting, adequately supported by fire, employed highly effective shock tactics. This will be represented by a shock bonus when the Swedish horse makes mêlée contact.
4 In the long term Swedish morale was higher than that of their enemy.
5 Perhaps greater than anything else, they were blessed by the immense morale-raising presence of their leader, Gustavus Adolphus.

When planning this reconstruction, it is not important to scale down actual numbers of men so long as there is a formation (regiment, brigade etc) on the table top for each one of those on the actual battlefield in 1631.

Set up both armies in their historical dispositions, then adopt the scenario shown.

| Phase | Swedes | Imperialists |
|---|---|---|
| 1 | Set up Skirmish Army moves forward Cannonade (incl Saxons) | Set up Skirmish Take cannonade and reply |
| 2 | Prepare to repel cavalry | |
| | | Cavalry charges on both flanks |
| | Move cavalry from Baner to form new front | |
| | Swedish cavalry counter-charges as guns/muskets fire | Pappenheim's cavalry charges until morale breaks, or pushed back by Swedish cavalry |
| | Saxons break | Croat cavalry pursues (two-move contact?) |
| 3 | Change front. | Tilly marches centre |
| | Reinforced 2 Bdes inf from centre 2$^{nd}$ line | Inf on Swedish exposed left flank Croats Cavalry mêlées return |
| | Cavalry mêlées with fire support Push of pike | Push of pike |
| 4 | 4 Cavalry regts from right charge forward up hill towards guns | Mêlées |

**Classification of Commanders**

Gustavus Adolphus is 'above average' and Count Tilly 'average'.

The Swedish sub-commanders Baner, Horn and Torstensson can also be rated 'above average', while Pappenheim, Furstenberg and Isolani will be 'average'. For the considerably smaller Swedish army to achieve victory in this battle reconstruction, it is necessary, and not unreasonable, to follow this course.

**Quality of Troops**

There will be no argument about grading the table-top Saxons second-class — a necessary factor (backed by historical precedent) if they are to follow the ignominious example of the troops they represent and flee the field at the beginning of the battle.

So marked was the superiority of the Swedes in all departments that they might well be wholly classified as 'elite', but, while this would undoubtedly aid in achieving the historical result, such a mass upgrading might unbalance the wargame, besides making it difficult to find a wargamer who would take on the unrewarding role of Count Tilly. The situation can be handled in one of two ways — by classifying as 'elite' a certain proportion of the Swedish units (25 per cent of the cavalry units and 33 per cent of the infantry units, for example), or, better still, attempting to simulate the collective tactical brilliance and quality of the Swedish soldiers by nominating groups of Swedish foot, horse and artillery who will, when fighting together, have bonus points added to their firing and mêlée factors. Once a group is broken up and each arm is acting separately, these bonus points are not bestowed. This will realistically simulate the manner in which the Swedes joined together in closely knit combinations of foot/horse/guns, to form teams that were seemingly almost invincible in their day and age.

The excellence of Swedish firepower is repeatedly recorded, and wargames rules controlling rate of fire, accuracy and casualty-inflicting effect must enable them to be approximately double those of their Imperialist opponents. The extreme mobility of the Swedish formations is represented by allowing them a greater move-distance than the Imperialists. Brilliantly handled and excellently trained, they reacted quickly to situations and to orders — simulated by allowing Swedish reactions to unexpected situations (a flank attack, for example) to be instantaneous, whereas the same reaction on the part of an Imperialist force would take up a third or half their move-distance.

The presence of Gustavus Adolphus undoubtedly had a marked effect upon the men he was leading and who could see him during the battle. That effect can be allowed for by giving a points bonus to their fighting qualities on such occasions.

What of the Imperialists? Solid, well trained and experienced troops, they were unfortunate to come up against the outstanding commander of his day, leading a superb and confident army following tactics that were far superior to their own cumbrous and outmoded manoeuvres. In all fairness the Imperialists rate the classification of 'average', their numerical superiority being balanced by the suggested 'fighting bonuses' bestowed upon the Swedes. Pappenheim's cavalry must have been composed of first-class troops to throw themselves seven times upon the Swedes, in the face of heavy musketry and artillery fire and cavalry counter-charges, before being finally thrown back.

**Morale**

The Swedes must be given morale bonuses when their different arms are working in close cooperation with the remainder of their 'team'. As their long-term morale was better than that of the enemy, a progressively decreasing standard of morale can be used for the Imperialists, although the usual morale penalties incurred through combat reverses may be considered sufficient. The presence of

**Wargame Terrain for BREITENFELD**

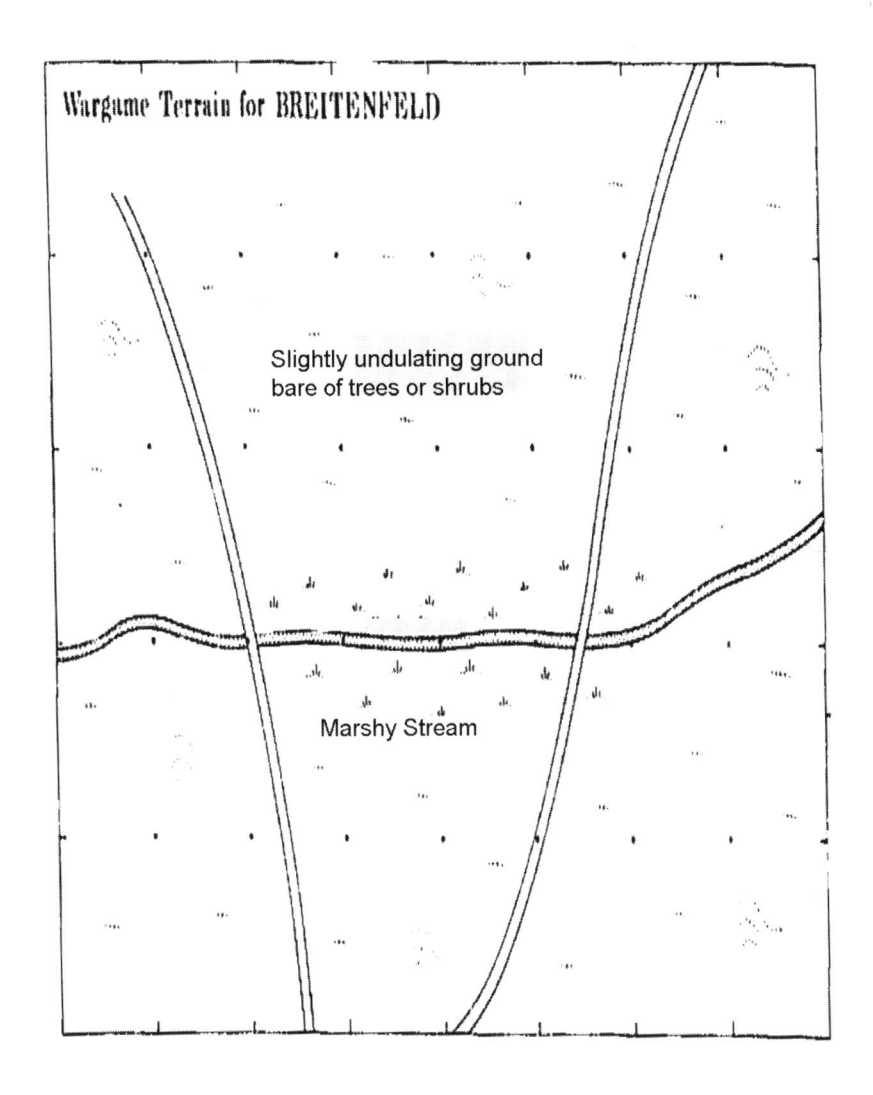

Slightly undulating ground bare of trees or shrubs

Marshy Stream

Gustavus Adolphus with a unit should allow bonus points to be added to the morale rating of that unit and to those who are able to see him.

Gustavus personally led a cavalry charge on the Imperialist guns in the later stages of the battle and, as even a novice wargamer soon learns, it is a rather foolhardy business to charge guns with cavalry, even on a table-top battlefield! Under normal wargames rules Gustavus's cavalry charge would probably have been turned back because morale would have fallen under heavy casualties. However, the fact remains that Gustavus and his cavalry did successfully charge batteries of guns. The rules, therefore, must be slanted to allow for such eventualities: for example, the presence of Gustavus himself could add a morale bonus to the already high morale of his cavalry.

Summing up, the initial morale of the entire Swedish force must be first-class *plus*. That of the Saxons will be second-class at the outset, soon dropping to third-class. The morale of the Imperialist force will initially be first-class.

All the morale will fluctuate, in the usual manner, in accordance with combat eventualities.

### Effect and Construction of Terrain
This was a perfectly straightforward battle on an ideal arena, unaffected by the small stream running between the two armies and the slight undulations of the bare and treeless plain. Its construction is simplicity itself and, in point of fact, it is a terrain that enables the battle to represent an ideal tactical exercise for the Pike-and-Shot period.

### Military Possibilities
It would seem that there are few Military Possibilities that could have altered circumstances to present a different result.

If the Saxons on the Swedish left had held, it would have only enabled Gustavus to win even more easily and decisively. The uncovered Swedish flank might have broken, but the mobility of the troops there, in contrast to the ponderous movement of the tercios, made this most unlikely.

Pappenheim's cavalry charges with his Black Cuirassiers might have broken the Swedish right, but even had they done so, experiences in this and other battles indicate that the mobility and fluid tactics of the Swedes would have plugged the gap and averted defeat. In any event, it would be unrealistic for either of the Swedish flanks to break in this reconstruction.

## 11. The Battle of Lützen 16 November 1632

WALLENSTEIN, THE Imperialist leader, marching his army into Saxony pursued by Gustavus Adolphus and his Swedes, had entrenched a winter camp along the line of the Leipzig-Lutzen road. His right was anchored on the village of Liitzen, which fronted Windmill Hill, the only rising ground in a gently rolling plain, where most of the Imperial guns were posted. It was a position that neutralised the Swedish mobility and forced them to attack frontally, as the straight causeway road, lined with ditches deepened into trenches for the musketeers, gave no room for the type of manoeuvres that brought victory at Breitenfeld. Hearing that Pappenheim with 8,000 men, mostly cavalry, was away seeking provisions, Gustavus decided to move against the position, but the early autumn dusk prevented an immediate attack and both armies faced each other in line of battle throughout a long, damp and chilly night.

In much the same formation as at Breitenfeld the 20,000-strong Swedish army was commanded by Gustavus on the right, and Duke Bernard of Saxe-Weimar, a German Protestant with a reputation for bravery, on the left. The two lines of infantry each had 4 brigades of foot in their centre, commanded by General Niels Brahe and by the veteran Marshal Kniphausen. Torstensson was in charge of the artillery — 20 large pieces in the centre and 40 light regimental guns divided between the wings.

Wallenstein hastily recalled Pappenheim and his 8,000 men (for whom an area was kept open on the left flank), and formed up the Imperial army of about 22,000 men along the line of the Leipzig road. Lutzen was fired so that it could not be used as cover. The infantry in the centre were drawn up in four great oblong masses, solid blocks of Spanish (or Spanish-trained) pikemen in the old tercio formation, with musketeers thrust out at each corner, and other infantry formations were placed near Lutzen. Cavalry were stationed on the flanks of the main body of infantry, Piccolomini commanding the Austrian and Hungarian cuirassiers opposite Gustavus. Colloredo was in command of the foot and horse supporting the 14 guns on Windmill Hill, and the rest of the artillery (7 guns) was placed in front of the centre, Skirmishers (detached from the musketeers of the tercios) lined the ditch before the main body.

Forced to make a frontal attack, Gustavus planned that Duke Bernard with the cavalry of the left should attack Lutzen while he, with a reinforced right wing, would crush the opposing left wing, cutting Wallenstein's line of retreat to Leipzig. Heavy fog and smoke from the burning village prevented the guns from firing until mid-morning, when, aided by their stabs of flame throwing bright orange flashes through the gloom, the two armies began groping for each other.

In the general Swedish advance along the whole line their mobile infantry in the centre reached the double-ditched road, exchanging fire with the skirmishers; then Torstensson brought up the light regimental guns and their enfilade fire soon caused the musketeers in the ditches to abandon their position. Surging across the road, the Swedish infantry overran the Imperial artillery positions, capturing the big immobile guns and spiking them, then pressed on to attack the massive blocks of pikemen positioned behind the guns. Deprived of their musketeers by the fighting along the road, these squares, still in formation and with their right anchored, were forced slowly back on the left. At the same time both Gustavus and Bernard were pressing forward. On the right the Swedish leader at the head of his veteran Stalhanske cavalry scattered a group of Croat light cavalry and brushed aside a solid mass of cuirassiers, which were then routed by successive waves of Swedish cavalry. On the Swedish left Duke Bernard of Saxe-Wcimar, although he was overlapped and had a hill to climb, and in spite of Wallenstein taking personal command, succeeded in leading some of Brahe's men up Windmill Hill and capturing its big battery of artillery.

At this stage Gustavus, who had pulled out too far right in the restricting fog of battle, received word that Wallenstein had successfully counterattacked with pikemen and cavalry against the right flank of Brahe's infantry line, hitting them at a moment when they were disorganised by their own cavalry dismounting to lead their horses across the ditches. Hastening across to the threatened area, Gustavus outgalloped all but four of his men, and rode out of the mist straight into a party of the enemy, who shot them down, killing Gustavus and three others. As word spread that the King's riderless horse had been seen galloping from the field, the Swedish advance lost momentum. At the same time, out of the mist on to the extreme end of Brahe's line, a series of charges by Piccolomini's heavy cavalry rolled it up, recapturing the seven spiked guns and throwing the Swedes back to the road, where they lost first one ditch then the other.

After angrily rejecting advice from old Marshal Kniphausen that their second line of foot should cover a retreat, Duke Bernard took command of the Swedish army. Riding down the lines crying, 'Swedes! They have killed the King!' above the noise of gunfire, he kindled a new fury in the Swedish soldiers, so that they forgot their exhaustion and surged forward in a fresh advance.

After some hard riding, Pappenheim and his 8,000 cavalry had reached the field, and moved across towards the shattered Imperialist left. Near Wallenstein's baggage park they rode out of the mist to charge the Swedish right-wing cavalry, who, lacking orders and with their leader dead, had halted indecisively. The newly arrived horsemen crashed into the much smaller stationary squadrons to send them reeling back across the causeway. Then Pappenheim was killed, and the surge of his counterattack, died with him.

About five o'clock, with the coming of dusk, Swedish fortunes began to turn when the mist cleared, so that Torstensson was able to get his guns going again; at the same time the captured Windmill Hill battery was able to enfilade the enemy and prevent them from crossing the

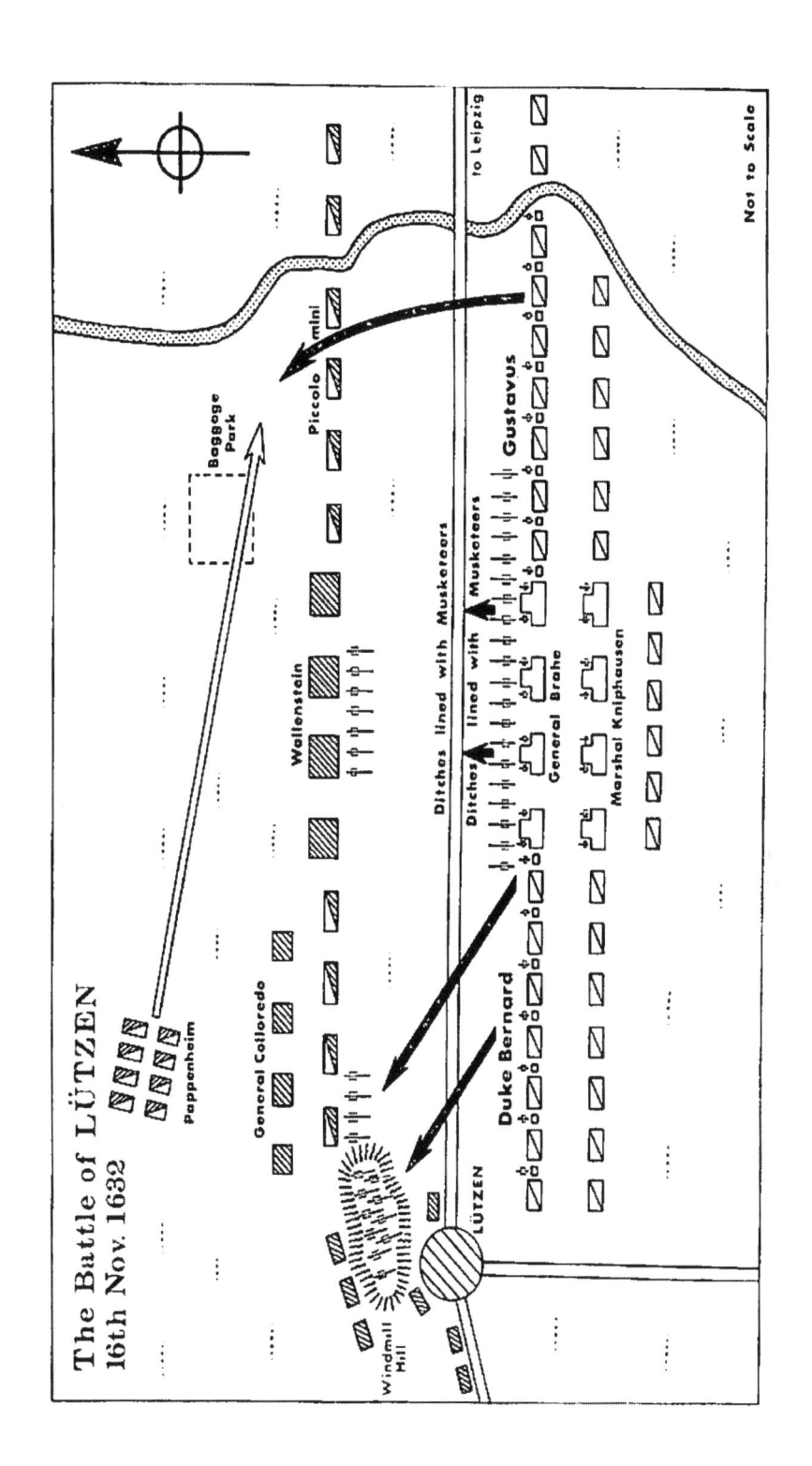

# The Battle of LÜTZEN
## 16th Nov. 1632

road. The Imperialist centre battery was unable to return fire because the guns were still spiked. At this, the most desperate moment of the battle, there was little thought of tactics as desperate hand-to-hand combats took place between small groups of men. Although painfully wounded, Bernard harnessed the fury of the 'fighting-mad' Swedes to send them sweeping forward in a desperate and irresistible assault that drove the Imperialists from the field.

Wallenstein withdrew the shattered remnants of his army to Halle. With 12,000 casualties, it was not so much beaten as destroyed, some companies being reduced to two or three survivors and the whole of the artillery and baggage lost. The Swedish army had also suffered heavily, losing about 10,000 men; some of its brigades were reduced to one-sixth of their original strength.

**Reconstructing the Battle as a Wargame**
The principal, and most elusive, aspect that has to be simulated in this reconstruction is the effect of the fog on all movements. Much of what happened, including the death of Gustavus Adolphus, was influenced by it, and its easing at 5pm allowed the Swedes to clinch the victory. Surprise and concealment, and their consequent uncertainty, are among the most difficult factors to simulate on the wargames table, but, when reconstructing a battle where these aspects play a key part, their realistic simulation is essential.

The simplest way of representing the effect of fog is to specify a definite vision distance (say 9 inches), so that beyond that distance no counteraction may be taken by one side to a move of the other's. It can be laid down that all combatants must expend a certain proportion of a game-move in assessing a situation — for example, an infantry formation cannot prepare themselves for a cavalry attack coming in on their flank until they have expended the prescribed proportion of the game-move in weighing up the situation and issuing the necessary orders for counteraction. As suggested in the Breitenfeld reconstruction, the tactical sharpness of the Swedes is simulated by allowing them a shorter assessment period than the Imperialists. Under these foggy conditions the Swedes should take half a game-move to assess a situation, whereas the Imperialists take a complete game-move to do the same thing. This will work when applied by "friendly' wargamers, who prize the enjoyment of the game above the victory, but when more ambitious contestants are concerned, the following method leaves fewer loopholes for acrimony.

The wargamers representing Gustavus Adolphus and Wallenstein are each given a scaled map of the battlefield covered by talc or transparent plastic, which will take the markings of a chinagraph wax pencil. Instead of writing down on an order sheet the direction of a unit's move or performing the act directly on the table, each commander marks the movement on his map by means of an arrow extending over the scaled-down distance of the move. When the game begins, each commander marks on his map the historical dispositions of his army; then both mark in the first game-move, neither knowing what the other has written. Each map is now passed to an umpire, who, by placing the transparent talc sheets on top of each other, with a map of the terrain underneath, is able to detect whether any formations are within sight of each other or have actually come into contact. When this occurs, the umpire marks on the map those enemy forces visible to each other, and the respective commanders place those units on the table-top battlefield, continuing in this manner until all units are on the table and in full view. The umpire must keep a tight hand on proceedings, as it might be necessary to remove formations from the table and alter map markings should units pass beyond the enemy's line of vision. At Lutzen the fog lifted about 5pm (about three-quarters of the way through the battle), and from that time on the umpire will allow the battle to become a normal wargame, with both commanders enjoying their usual godlike field of vision over the whole field.

A restricted field of vision will naturally handicap gunners and musketeers, but it will not cut short the range of their weapons, so that there will be an 'effective' firing range and a 'blind' firing range, the former being much more lethal than the latter. With the weapons of the period taking perhaps a complete game-move to reload, both artillerymen and musketeers can be caught with unloaded weapons if they have fired in the previous move; and it may well happen that enemy forces will emerge from the mist at these crucial moments. Such circumstances may have allowed the Swedes to approach the ditches, perhaps only taking a single volley, before Torstensson was able to bring up his light guns and drive out the defenders. Similarly, the Swedish infantry may have reached the guns in the Imperialist centre without taking so much fire as to be driven back.

During this part of the battle it is recorded that the Imperialist guns were spiked. This was probably done as soon as the guns were overrun, or it can be ruled that it will take a specified number of men a prescribed part of a game-move to carry out the task. Presumably these central Imperialist guns were put out of action because it was considered quite likely that they would be recaptured. The guns on Windmill Hill were not spiked, presumably because the Swedes considered that, having taken the hill, they were unlikely to lose it, and the guns could be turned against their former owners.

An integral part of the battle was the Imperialists' counterattack in the centre, which was successful because the Swedish infantry were thrown into confusion when their cavalry passed through them, dismounted, to negotiate the ditch. This may be simulated by allowing the Swedish cavalry to take a specified part of a move to cross the ditch, and by devising 'local' rules to cause disorder.

The deaths of Gustavus Adolphus and Pappenheim must be simulated at the appropriate stages of the battle, because they both bore on its eventual outcome. The death of the Swedish leader 'froze' his cavalry, with disastrous results, and a 'local' rule should ensure that they remain halted, near Wallenstein's baggage park, until joined by another leader. Pappenheim's death caused his cavalry's counterattack to peter out when it showed signs of turning the whole course of the battle. This factor can be controlled by a morale rule arising from the death of a leader. A morale rule of the opposite sort will handle the remarkably successful manner in which Duke Bernard rallied the Swedes and transformed their grief into fury. This strong emotion can be represented on the wargames table by awarding the Swedes a bonus of increased move-distance and fighting ability, using percentage dice to discover if Bernard's chance of maintaining Swedish morale at peak is 60 per cent, say, or perhaps 75 per cent, and by adjusting fighting standards as the percentage drops.

**Classification of Commanders**

Gustavus Adolphus was undoubtedly 'above average' and Bernard, if only because he kept the Swedes in the battle and won it, can share this classification. The Imperialist leaders Wallenstein and Pappenheim should, by comparison, be classified as 'average'.

**Quality of Troops**

As at Breitenfeld, the Swedish troops were all first-class and the rulings applied in this earlier battle will serve as a guide for Lutzen. The Imperialists were of average quality.

The use of the revolutionary Swedish tactics against the 'period' but outmoded tactics of the Imperialists should ensure the historically victorious side achieving a table-top success. The Swedes should be classified as suggested in the Breitenfeld notes, or else Bernard's predominantly cavalry attack against the batteries on Windmill Hill, for example, would probably be thrown back. This also applies in other circumstances, such as the Swedish attack on the musketeers lining the ditches.

The same rules and conditions concerning the Swedish rate of fire will apply at Lutzen as they did in the Breitenfeld reconstruction.

**Morale**

The morale of both sides was first-class at the onset, and fluctuated according to the eventualities of combat. The Swedes had superior long-term morale, as exemplified in the notes for the previous battle.

Seemingly Pappenheim's cavalry were much affected by his death, and this must be reflected in the morale rules under which they operate. If this is not done, their progress could change the course of the battle. When Gustavus was killed, the manner in which Duke Bernard of Saxe-Weimar rallied the Swedish troops, transforming their grief into 'battle-madness', can be simulated by balancing their normal high morale with a 'grief' deduction. This is represented by a chain reaction running from unit to unit, as the news of the King's death spreads through the army. The 'battle-fury' of the Swedes can be likened to an 'uncontrolled charge' brought about by a morale dice throw that raises morale even above first-class standard.

# Wargame Terrain for LÜTZEN

*Flossgraben Stream*

*Ditch*

*Ditch*

*Windmill Hill*

**LÜTZEN**
(Burning)

### Effect and Construction of Terrain

The nature of the terrain and the Imperialist positions forced the Swedes to attack frontally, depriving them of opportunities for their usual highly efficient tactical manoeuvring. Windmill Hill and the ditches lining the road favoured the Imperialists, both playing an important part in the course and outcome of the battle.

This is a simple terrain to construct, being flat apart from Windmill Hill. The village of Lutzen can be represented, although it plays no tactical role other than to add smoke to the fog.

Digging ditches in a solid-topped wargames table is difficult, and it is not really important whether the musketeers shelter in ditches or behind banks. A certain degree of licence can be taken by lining the road with earth banks or stone walls.

### Military Possibilities

These revolve almost entirely around the fog, which was responsible, for instance, for such events as the death of Gustavus Adolphus, which would not have happened under normal visual conditions.

If Pappenheim with his 8,000 cavalry had been in position on the Imperialist left wing at the start of the battle, the charge of Gustavus might well have been less successful. On the other hand, if one is to judge by such previous battles as Breitenfeld, it took a great deal to stop the Swedish cavalry in full flight when led by their King! Pappenheim's cavalry could have altered the entire outcome of the battle if his death had not destroyed their momentum.

If the attacking Swedes had not spiked the guns of the Imperialist centre battery, these guns might well have been used to advantage when recaptured. On the other hand, if they had remained unspiked, they could have been turned by the Swedes, with devastating effect, against the solid masses of the tercios.

It is possible that Swedish fortunes might have taken a different turn had the fog not lifted in the late afternoon, to allow Torstensson to use his artillery to full effect. But this was historical reality at a decisive moment in the battle, and should not be changed if realism is to be maintained.

## 12. The Battle of Rocroi 19 May 1643

IN ITS twenty-sixth year, with all the old leaders dead and the major military action shifting from Germany to north-eastern France, the Thirty Years War had developed into a power struggle between the House of Bourbon and the Spanish/Austrian Hapsburgs. In spring 1643 General Francisco de Melo was besieging Rocroi, an important frontier fortress on the line of the Meuse. To its relief marched the twenty-two year-old Duc d'Enghien (later the 'Great Conde') with 15.000 infantry and 7.000 cavalry. After centuries of relying largely on mercenaries, the French, following their reorganisation by Richelieu, at last had what could possibly be called a French army. De Melo's army had 6 Spanish tercios (10,000 men), composed of the usual formidable veterans, and the remaining 8,000 infantry comprised Flemish, Walloon, Italian and mercenary contingents, with their own leaders but officered by Spaniards. Their, well mounted cavalry force under the Comte d'Isembourg consisted of 8,000 excellent horsemen. At this date the Spanish armies could generally be considered superior to the French.

Enghien's most trusted commander, the Comte de Gassion, reported that to attack the Spaniards the French army had to march through a narrow marsh-ridden rocky defile to reach a plateau four miles wide and surrounded by thickets and heavy undergrowth. Nevertheless, he advised battle, though L'Hopital, an older and more cautious military adviser, wished to avoid a confrontation. In the event the French marched out, and at 8am on the 18th the heads of their columns reached the fringe of the plateau, to find the approaches unguarded and their route through the woods opposed only by outposts that scattered before them. It has been said that de Melo wished to surround and take the whole French army rather than put it to flight. Pushing ahead, Enghien suddenly saw, in an open space between the surrounding forests, the whole Spanish array drawn up in the conventional formation of right, centre and left, with musketeers filling the gaps between cavalry squadrons, so that it looked like a single block. The Spanish tercios formed the centre, in front of a second line of allied foot, and the cavalry were divided equally between the two wings. In the manner of the day, the artillery was placed out in front of the infantry.

Emerging on to open ground, the French were so formed that the movements and numbers of their infantry were concealed by their advancing cavalry, in front and on both flanks. By 6pm Enghien had drawn up his troops within cannon shot of the Spaniards. He personally commanded the right wing, which was formed of cavalry and faced a Spanish cavalry force under the Duke of Albuquerque, though separated from them by a thin strip of woodland occupied by Spanish musketeers. The French left wing, commanded by L'Hopital and Sennetere, opposed de Melo himself with a force of horsemen,

**The Battle of ROCROI**
**19th May 1643**

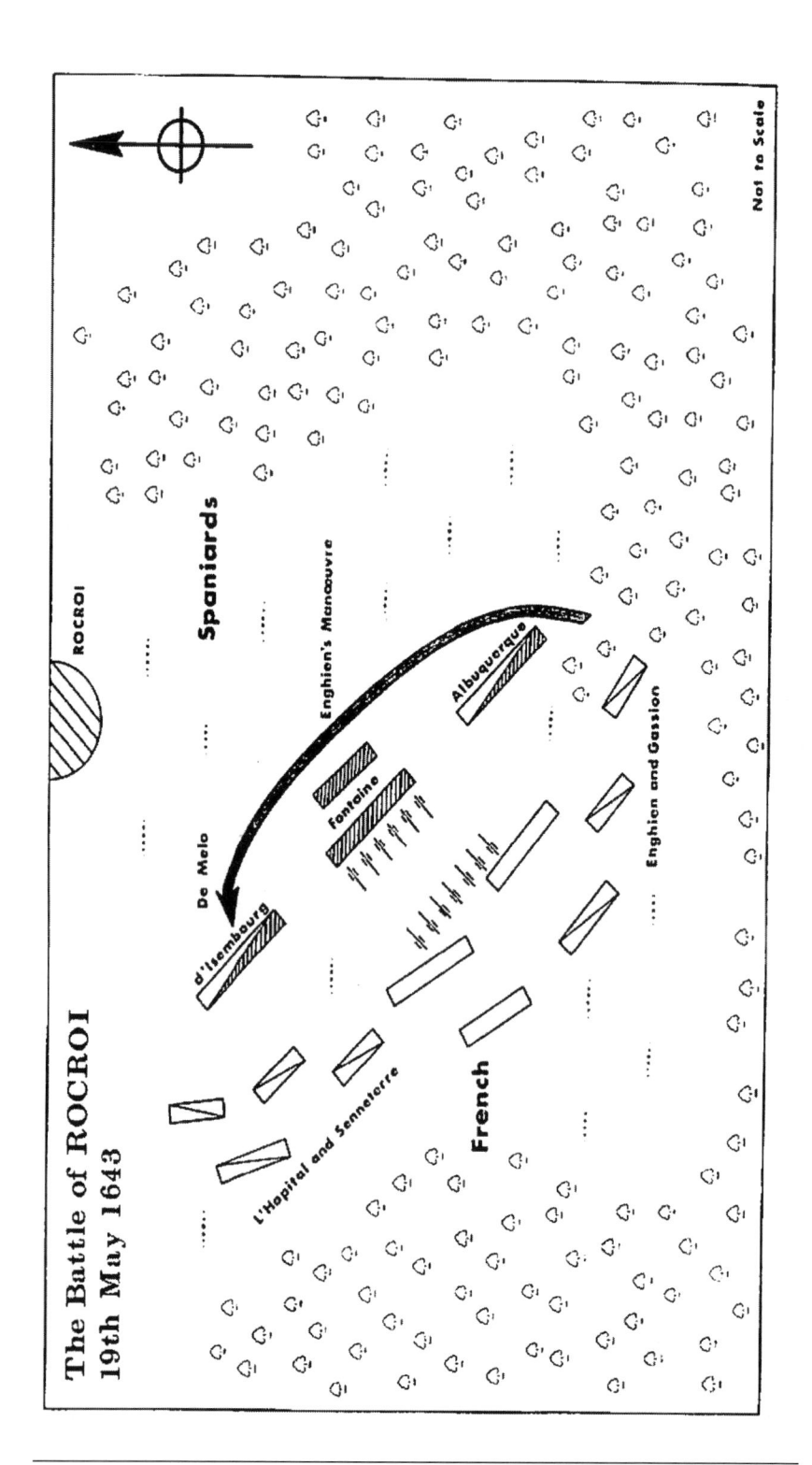

Not to Scale

ROCROI

Spaniards

De Melo
Enghien's Manoeuvre
Fontaine
Albuquerque
d'Isembourg

L'Hopital and Senneterre
Enghien and Gassion

French

while the Spanish infantry were commanded by the veteran Flemish general, Fontaine. After a premature advance by Senneterre had almost brought disaster to the French, both armies settled down for the night.

Arising at 3am, the French formed up, and in the half light of dawn Enghien's cavalry wing, comprising his own 8 squadrons and 7 led by Gassion, drove the Spanish musketeers out of the woodland and fell upon Albuquerque's cavalry. The Spaniards' first line was taken in flank and scattered by Enghien's 'wild and ferocious' Croat horsemen, and when the experienced Spanish cavalry leader rallied his second line, it was immediately driven back in great disorder and with heavy losses by Enghien's horse frontally and Gassion's on the flank, in a display of almost unparalleled speed of action.

With Gassion's cavalry pursuing the fugitives, Enghien surveyed the battlefield, now wreathed in billowing clouds of smoke, but he could see that his left wing was in trouble. L'Hopital and Senneterre, charging before being ordered, had been repulsed and were falling back in disorder after being charged by d'Isembourg and his Spanish cavalry, which had spent the night close up behind their infantry and were able to jump straight into a gallop. After routing the French horse and cutting them off from the infantry in the centre, the Spanish cavalry swerved left to rout the musketeers guarding the artillery and capture the guns. A counter attack by L'Hopital won back a few pieces, but then lost them again, so that the Spanish had 30 guns to bombard the French centre, which had none to answer them. The French infantry, outnumbered and outmatched, could only stand on the defensive against the Spanish infantry.

Now Gassion, who had returned from the pursuit, was ordered to remain in case Albuquerque rallied, while Enghien wheeled his 8 squadrons left and, at the gallop, rode behind the enemy's centre and began cutting a path through their massed infantry formations. He passed between the first Spanish tercio, hotly engaged with the French infantry, and the Italian, German and Walloon formations, which were struck in flank (in that order). The surprise assault broke the allied infantry, although the Italians fought magnificently and both their leaders were killed. Without drawing rein, Enghien's cavalry circled right round the field to come up on the rear of d'Isembourg's cavalry, which, caught between two enemy forces, broke to their right and fled the field.

All that remained were the Spanish tercios, veterans in solid formations but hemmed in on all sides. Could they hold out until reinforcements arrived? The French infantry advanced to within fifty paces, only to be broken and sent reeling back in disorder by controlled volleys of musketry fire. His men and horses exhausted, Enghien withdrew the most fatigued and, reinforcing the infantry with some cavalry, sent them in once more — again they were repulsed -- and then a third time. A charge by cavalry alone was also thrown back with heavy losses, and Enghien's horse was shot from under him.

Then Cassion came up and Senneterre returned from pursuit. After a short rest while the French artillery flayed the Spanish blocks, the weary and somewhat dispirited French cavalry made a third charge. This time not a Spanish gun fired on them and there was only a splattering of musketry — seemingly the Spanish had run out of ammunition. Enghien directed the cavalry into gaps made by his artillery, disorganising the Spanish infantry, so that when their commander, Fontaine, was killed by a stray shot and the French infantry closed in, the Spaniards surrendered. Unfortunately the excited French mistook a Spanish movement to be a renewal of resistance, fighting broke out again and, before Enghien and his officers could halt the massacre, the flower of the Spanish army had been cut down. The total Spanish losses were 7,000 dead and 6,000 prisoners, nearly all of them wounded. The French suffered 4,000 casualties.

Enghien's victory was won by his generalship and his calculated risk in cutting through the Spanish centre. So ended a battle that destroyed the legend of Spanish invincibility. Rocroi was a turning point in Spanish military history, for never again could Spain produce infantry the equal of those who fell there.

**Reconstructing the Battle as a Wargame**
Provided there is an accurate scaling down of the numerical disparity (cavalry French 7:8 infantry French 15:18), there is no need to worry about actual numbers, though each formation of Rocroi must be represented on the table top.

Initially set up the troops in the historical dispositions as at dawn on 19th May. The battle will begin when Enghien and Gassion attack the musketeers in the wood and rout them, so allowing the French horse to come quickly upon Albuquerque's cavalry, probably catching them at the halt. The Spaniards were further distracted during the frontal cavalry attack of Enghien by Gassion, who had gone through the woods and seen off the musketeers, coming in on the flank of their first line. The second line, affected and disordered by their fleeing comrades passing through them, was also routed by the French cavalrymen, who retained the impetus from their original charge.

As they had done on the previous night, the French left-wing cavalry attacked without orders — on the table in the game-move immediately following that heralding the start of Enghien's attack. The precipitate left-wing charge hits part of d'Isembourg's cavalry front, but the rest of his command is stationed behind its nearest infantry formation, so that it is able to come in without warning on the flank of the attacking French force. Normal wargames rules will probably cause the French to be defeated here, as in real life.

Now comes the most difficult reconstruction of all — that of Enghien's feat in cutting right through the opposing infantry. For reasons of realism, this must be given a high chance of succeeding, and can be worked by having the front rank of the infantry move forward into mêlée contact with the French infantry, causing a gap between them and their second line. Through this gap Enghien's cavalry strikes the Italian formation (the first he encounters) in flank, causing it to retreat, into the next formation, so disordering that one — while the French cavalry continue to advance. Enghien should be successful with normal wargames rules controlling elite cavalry attacking second-class infantry, plus the bonuses for flank attacks and a disordered enemy. Emerging from this attack, Enghien and his cavalry plunge into the rear of d'Isembourg, who, engaged both in front and rear, not unexpectedly flees the field.

The six Spanish tercios remain and, being elite troops, they will easily repulse the attacks of the second-rate French infantry, and also the other infantry/cavalry attacks that follow. The battle proceeds until Enghien does the sensible tactical thing and turns on them the close-range massed fire of both his own and the captured Spanish guns. Presumably these guns only fired for about one game-move, or the losses they inflicted would have been sufficient to cause even elite troops to break through failing morale.

The French cavalry charge that finally caused the tercios to surrender was successful to a large extent because the Spanish had run out of ammunition. This can be simulated on the wargames table by rationing the guns and musketeer formations to, say, five or six shots per game; then, by noting each shot as it is fired, it can be discovered when they have run out of ammunition. This seemingly small ration is relative to other scaled-down factors used in reproducing a real battle on a table-top terrain.

Another method is to rule that it takes a complete game-move for a gun (and musketeers) to reload, whereas firing takes no time at all. Therefore a force that fired in game-move No 6 will, if charged in game-move No 7, be unable to fire on its attackers. It could well have happened that the Spanish artillery replied to the French barrage, so that the guns were empty for the charge-move. Alternatively, the morale of the tercios might not be quite high enough to withstand the effects of massed artillery fire followed by a cavalry charge.

**Classification of Commanders**
Enghien and Gassion are undoubtedly 'above average', but L'Hopital and Senneterre are 'below average'. The Spanish commander, de Melo, can be classified as 'average', as can Albuquerque and Fontaine, but d'Isembourg, because of his success on the Spanish right, could be given an 'above average' rating.

**Quality of Troops and Morale**
The French cavalry of Enghien and Gassion can be classified as 'elite', Senneterre's cavalry as 'average', and the French infantry as 'below average'.

The Spanish tercios were 'elite' troops but their Italian, Walloon and German allies were 'below average', since Enghien was able to break through them. The musketeers in the wood, scattered by the French right-wing cavalry, would seemingly also be 'below average', or they would have held their own, aided as they were by woods and undergrowth. The Spanish cavalry were 'average'.

To some extent the morale classification of a formation of troops is related to its quality, so that 'elite' troops are given a bonus when deciding their state of morale, whereas 'below average' troops suffer a deduction.

Throughout the course of the battle the initial morale classification will fluctuate according to the eventualities of battle.

### Effect and Construction of Terrain

Once the French were through the defile, the battle was fought on a largely open plateau. The only part of the surrounding woods that had a role in the battle was that in front of Albuquerque, from which Gassion's cavalrymen drove the musketeers, and from which they emerged unexpectedly on the flank of the first line of Spanish cavalry. Wargames rules usually preclude cavalry from acting successfully in woods, but in this case, as the musketeers of history put up a poor show, the trees should be sparse so that the area is a mere clearing through which cavalry can move. When constructing the wargames terrain, it might be best to line the edges of the table with trees, symbolically indicating the surrounding forest. Otherwise the ground is completely flat with just a small spur of trees (a clearing) extending a little in from one end of the table.

### Military Possibilities

So tightly balanced was this French victory that almost any permitted Military Possibility can change the historical result. For example, if Enghien had not thrown the musketeers out of the wood and taken Albuquerque's cavalry by surprise, he would not have been in a position to make his reckless but decisive dash through the centre of the Spanish infantry. And if that cavalry charge had failed, as well it might, the Spanish would almost certainly have won.

If L'Hopital had not precipitately advanced on the left, there would have been no need for Enghien to make his charge. The French left might have been successful, however, if d'Isembourg's cavalry had not been poised to hit them. Had d'Isembourg's cavalry gone on to destroy the French left and move left round to the rear of the French positions before the arrival of Enghien, it might have provided a situation in which two large cavalry forces each tried to catch the other's tail!

If the French infantry in the centre had broken and fled before the Spanish tercios became isolated, these solid formations of veteran troops would have been quite capable of holding off the battle-weary French cavalry, particularly if they had held on to more of their artillery and adequate supplies of ammunition.

Had Gassion not come across and Senneterre not returned from the pursuit, to aid the final charge, Enghien might well have found his tired and dispirited troops incapable of taking advantage of the casualties caused by his artillery upon the still-formed Spanish tercios.

# 13. The Battle of Cropredy Bridge 29 June 1644

IN EARLY summer 1644 Charles I and his army, watched by Waller's Parliamentary army, was engaged in a series of marches and manoeuvres in Oxfordshire. On 29 June, after a small skirmish at Crouch near Banbury, the two armies were marching on parallel lines on either side of the River Cherwell, in sight of one another, although out of musket shot. The Royalist army was in three divisions: the van led by Lord Wilmot; the main body, with the King and the Prince of Wales; the rearguard comprising Colonel Thelwell and 1,000 foot, and the Lords Northampton and Cleveland, each with a brigade of horse. The Parliamentary army reached Cropredy Bridge, where the river bent sharply north-east and was crossed two miles further on at Hays Bridge by the Banbury/Daventry road. The distance between the two armies led the Royalists to believe that they would not be attacked; nevertheless a party of Royalist dragoons are said to have been sent to hold Cropredy Bridge until the army had passed beyond it.

The vanguard had crossed Hays Bridge when they heard that some 300 enemy horsemen were less than two miles ahead. The Royal Horse were sent after them, followed by the infantry of the vanguard, who proceeded without orders, and the main body crossed the bridge and joined the pursuit. But the rearguard maintained its original pace and a considerable gap developed between it and the main body — by the time the rearguard neared Cropredy Bridge the interval had lengthened to one and a half miles. Waller saw his chance of cutting off the Royalist rear and rushed Cropredy Bridge with two columns consisting of 8 troops of Hazlerig's regiment of horse ('The Lobsters') and 6 troops of Vandruske's regiment, totalling some 1,500 troopers, supported by 9 companies of infantry under Colonel Baines, 4 companies of Greencoats and 5 companies of Waller's own regiment. Eleven guns under James Wemyss, who had previously commanded Charles's guns but had defected to the Parliamentarians, were set up about three hundred yards north of the bridge, just clear of the river bank. Lieutenant-General Middleton, with 1,000 horse, crossed the river about a mile below the bridge at Slat Ford.

Once across the Cherwell, Hazlerig's horse galloped wildly in pursuit of the Royalist foot regiments of the rearguard, now approaching Hays Bridge, who saw them coming and drew up facing them, lining the bridge with musketeers and overthrowing a carriage as a barricade. Seeing this, and with no supporting infantry nearer than half a mile, the Parliamentary cavalry decided discretion to be the better part of valour and retired in the direction of Cropredy Bridge. Vandruske's regiment, although charged by Cleveland with some of the rearguard Royalist cavalry, was able to rally after being supported by infantry, but Cleveland's sweeping charge had cut off from Cropredy Bridge about

1,000 Parliamentary infantry, who were in disorderly retreat when overtaken and escorted by Hazlerig's retiring troopers. Further south, Northampton and his horse boldly charged Middleton's cavalry and, although not inflicting heavy losses, forced them back to Slat Mill, where they remained for the rest of the engagement, evidently not fancying their chances of taking a second charge.

The van, now well beyond Hays Bridge, halted, and the King sent Lord Bernard Stuart with 100 Gentlemen of the King's Troop to aid the rearguard, now facing a second attack from the rallied Roundheads. Stuart came up to Cleveland and his cavalry, who were making a stand near a great ash tree (where the King had halted for refreshments some half an hour earlier), and the joint cavalry forces, in spite of considerable musketry and artillery fire, drove both Parliamentary foot and horse back over Cropredy Bridge in an untidy rabble. James Wemyss and his guns could not get away, and he was captured with 5 sakers, 1 12-pounder piece, 1 demi-culverin, 2 minions and 2 3-pounder pieces, besides other artillery equipment.

Waller retreated westward beyond the River Cherwell to take up a position on high ground near Bourton, leaving some foot and dragoons at Cropredy Bridge, as the Royalists did not pursue beyond that point, and at Slat Mill ford. But the King, apparently piqued by Waller's militancy, decided to capture Cropredy Bridge and Slat Mill, and a hot engagement took place on and around the bridge. Waller's men not only held off the Royalists but also recovered three pieces of their lost artillery, after managing to advance Birch, with the Kentish Regiment and Tower Hamlet regiments and two drakes, to the bridge. The Royalists had little trouble in crossing at the ford and taking Slat Mill.

Both armies faced each other from the opposite heights, the river and the water meadows lying between them. As night approached, the Royalist foot and horse were drawn down to the river below the ford, and cannon were fired upon the enemy horse drawn up on Bourton Hill, causing them to retire in disorder. Then the two armies fell silent and the engagement was broken off.

In this small but lively engagement the Roundheads appear to have misjudged their attack. Instead of cutting off the King's rearguard, they found themselves caught between two fires, and it seemed that the King, more by accident than design, had drawn the enemy over Cropredy Bridge and inflicted a sharp reverse upon them.

**Reconstructing the Battle as a Wargame**
As in the reconstruction of many other of the battles described in this book, the number of troops used is not important, as long as there is a formation on the wargames table to coincide with its historical counterpart. Although numbers on both sides are known, all that are required for this battle are those who were engaged in the water rmeadows and the area formed by the bend in the river.

# The Battle of CROPREDY BRIDGE
## 29th June 1644

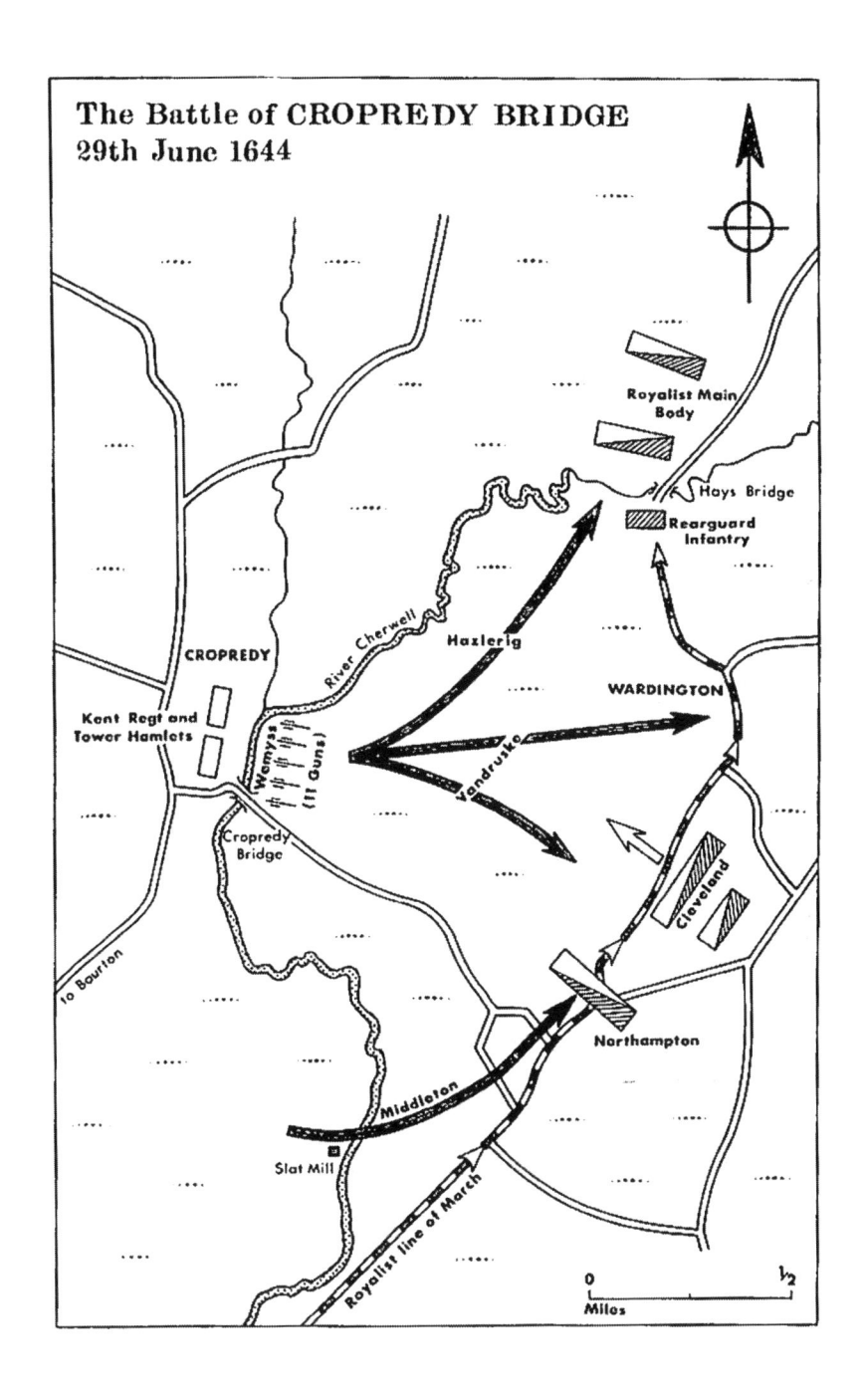

There is an element of surprise in Waller's attempt to pinch off the Royalist rearguard, although it depended on speed of movement, for the Royalists could see what he was doing. As a straightforward wargame, however, Cropredy Bridge forms an interesting engagement with considerable scope for cavalry manoeuvres.

The reconstruction begins with the wargamers representing the two commanders being told of the exact situation as it obtained in 1644. Set up Waller's Parliamentary army just beyond Cropredy Bridge, so that Hazlerig's and Vandruske's horsemen, with the infantry and Wemyss's guns, may cross the bridge to attack the Royalist rearguard. Middleton's cavalry will be just short of Slat Mill. The Royalist rearguard must be positioned on the table as it is on the terrain map, so that it will not be able to reach Hays Bridge and connect up with its infantry. Charles, with the main body, is beyond Hays Bridge and never comes on to the table, while the advance guard merely provides the reason for the gap in the Royalist column that precipitated the battle.

Once across the bridge, the Parliamentary cavalry, infantry and guns should logically go for their historical objectives. Hazlerig may actually attack the rearguard infantry who, if their wargame commander is at all dilatory, may not have reached the protection of Hays Bridge. The battle is one that can be allowed to proceed more or less as a normal wargame and, with the suggested troop quality and morale classifications, it should take a reasonably authentic course.

### Classification of Commanders

Waller, the Parliamentary commander, was at best 'average' but perhaps 'below average' here. Although Charles I was commanding the Royalist force, he never came on to the battlefield, nor did he exert any authority over the course of the action. For the Royalists, therefore, this was a soldiers' battle, local commanders acting on their own initiative. Thus, both Cleveland and Northampton can be classified 'above average' as both made the best of what could have been a bad situation.

For the Parliamentarians Hazlerig and Vandruske were 'average' commanders, and Middleton, who displayed neither initiative nor courage at Slat Mill, 'below average'. In the later stages of the battle it seems that Birch, for the Parliamentarians, displayed considerable courage and energy in bringing up the infantry that so easily held the bridge and recaptured some of the Parliamentary guns; although he was presumably acting under Waller's instructions, he can be classified as 'above average' for this local phase of the action.

### Quality of Troops and Morale

The Royalist cavalry of Northampton and Cleveland can be classified as 'elite' troops, as they displayed courage in holding off superior numbers. The Parliamentary cavalry of Hazlerig and Vandruske were 'average', as were the infantry who accompanied them, but Middleton's cavalry at Slat Mill were 'below average'. The Trained

Bands, the infantry that so ably defended Cropredy Bridge itself in the latter stage of the battle, should be given an 'elite' classification.

The state of morale of the contenders can be related to their quality, so that 'elite' troops are given a bonus when deciding their morale, 'average' troops test morale in the normal way, and those who are 'below average' have points deducted from their dice throw.

Morale will fluctuate according to circumstances, such as casualties, loss of leaders, lack of support etc.

**Effect and Construction of Terrain**

This is an interesting terrain needing careful construction, as it was the layout of the countryside, the river and the bridges, which made the battle possible. Both Cropredy and Hays Bridges were highly defensible, having stone parapets to shelter musketeers and only permitting a narrow defensive frontage, so equalising the numbers of attackers and defenders. The countryside over which the battle took place comprised flat water meadows and fields.

Its construction is not difficult but, just as the positioning of the initial layout of the Royalist rearguard makes for a successful battle, so does the accurate positioning of the river, the bridges and the ford. On the wargames map the river has been taken further to the right than on the actual battle map, so as to provide a larger field of action and avoid wasting a third of the terrain.

**Military Possibilities**

The slightest variations in distance can make an immense difference to this battle. For example, had the Royalist rearguard infantry been caught in the open by Hazlerig's cavalry on the way to Hays Bridge, they might have been destroyed and the cavalry regiments of Cleveland and Northampton would have been trapped, separated as they were from their comrades by Hazlerig's 'Lobsters'.

If Hazlerig had engaged the infantry at the bridge, the King's Gentlemen would not have been able to come to Cleveland's aid, and he would probably have been destroyed. In these circumstances, however, it is possible that Northampton would have noted Cleveland's precarious situation and come to his aid.

If Hazlerig's troopers, retreating from their abortive attempt to cut off the Royalist infantry rearguard, had not escorted the routed Parliamentary infantry, Cleveland might well have been able to rout them, and gone on to 'bounce' the bridge. On the other hand. Cleveland's cavalry, emerging on the Cropredy Bridge side of the routed Parliamentary infantry, could have run straight on to Wemyss' guns and been severely punished. These guns do not seem to have fired at any time, but they might have been masked by their own troops throughout the course of the battle.

If Wemyss's guns had been captured by the Royalists, they could have been turned on Birch's infantry, so ably defending Cropredy Bridge. This did not occur, either through lack of military foresight in that the Royalists surged forward to the attack without thinking to use the guns, or, much more likely, because the Royalists had no artillerymen with them. Finally, if Birch had failed to get the Trained Bands on to the Bridge to prevent it being captured by the Royalists, it is possible that a chain reaction might have spread among the remainder of Waller's force, so giving the Royalists a substantial victory.

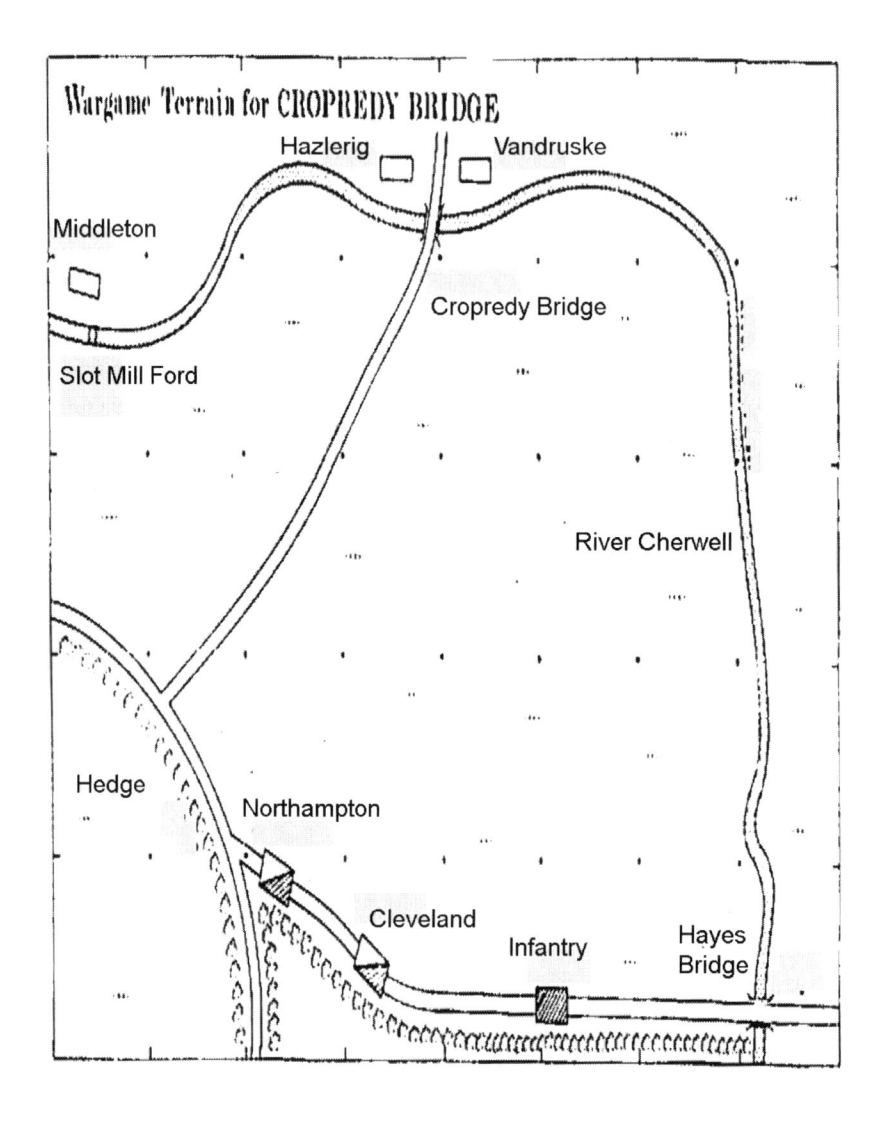

Wargame Terrain for CROPREDY BRIDGE

- Hazlerig
- Vandruske
- Middleton
- Cropredy Bridge
- Slot Mill Ford
- River Cherwell
- Hedge
- Northampton
- Cleveland
- Infantry
- Hayes Bridge

## 14. The Battle of Auldearn 9 May 1645

MANY AUTHORITIES consider the Battle of Auldearn, although it only involved small forces, to be the most brilliant battle of the English Civil War. It was a classic victory for the Marquis of Montrose, an outstanding commander of that period.

Under Colonel Sir John Hurry (later to turn his coat and serve under Montrose — both were executed in Edinburgh after the Carbisdale defeat in 1650) an English force was withdrawing to entice Montrose out of friendly hills and into Covenanter country. On the evening of 8 May, at the little village of Auldearn on a ridge of high treeless ground between the valleys of the Findhorn and the Nairn, Montrose posted his pickets carefully, pitched his camp and settled down for the night. His army, less than half the size of the English force, consisted of 250 horsemen under Louis Gordon and Lord James Aboyne, about 800 Irish under Alastair Colkitto MacDonald, and some 600 Highlanders.

Stealthily advancing towards Auldearn, Hurry lost the essential element of surprise when some of his men fired their muskets to clear out loaded charges, and Montrose's men heard the reports. In the little time remaining Montrose made hasty plans and dispositions. Alastair MacDonald, a physically strong man and a born leader with little time for tactics, was placed in command of a defensive flank with 250 men of an Irish regiment posted amid the gardens and enclosures of houses south of the church and 300 of the Gordon foot placed on the more easily defensible Castle Hill. MacDonald's line was about four hundred yards long. His men were instructed, by maintaining a continuous fire, to delude the enemy into thinking that the entire force was defending the village. Montrose wished to give the impression that he was personally in command in the centre of the position, at the south end of the Gordon foot in the angled line, so he planted ihe Royal Standard there. He concealed the rest of his infantry and the cavalry in a dip behind the crown of the ridge on his left wing. This force consisted of 800 infantry (2 Irish divisions and 100 Gordons) on the right, and on the left two bodies of horse, the right under Aboyne and the left under Lord Louis Gordon. The Royal force had no guns because its rapid marches of the past eight months had precluded recovery of the guns buried after the Battle of Aberdeen.

Montrose's dispositions, though hurried, were brilliant, for once the English were committed, he was free to swing his horse round from their cover and take the English in their right flank. Furthermore, the English cavalry would have decreased mobility among the village gardens if it attacked MacDonald thinking his force to be the entire Royal army.

Hurry deployed his force to advance in some depth on a narrow front — a good disposition for attacking a weaker force in a relatively unknown position — and left his artillery and waggon-train on the road. On the right was Lawer's regiment (directed against that part of the position held by MacDonald's Irish regiment); on the left was Loudoun's, its left flank hampered by the bog, advancing against the

Gordons on Castle Hill. These two regiments were supported by Lothian on the right and Buchanan on the left, and on the right of the Lothian regiment was the Moray horse (150 troopers under Drummond). In reserve from left to right were Seaforth's 600 strong Mackenzie contingent, the 500 Northern Levies and Sutherland's contingent of 500. Hurry's cavalry reserve of 250 remained in the rear, ready for pursuit or exploitation. The force totalled 2,000 regular and 1,600 local foot, with 400 horse and 9 guns.

The battle began with the impatient MacDonald, temperamentally unsuited to stand on the defensive, leaving the shelter of the enclosures to hurl his Irish at Lawer's regiment, which, with the help of Lothian's regiment, was able to force the Irish infantry back into the enclosures. Unable to take advantage of their superior numbers on this narrow front, however, the Covenanters could make no further headway against the outnumbered Irish who fought desperately among the pigsties and gardens of the village. Having observed these events from the crest of Castle Hill, Montrose ran across to the hollow on his left from where Gordon's unseasoned horse could see nothing of the fight in the village. It was essential that they be sent into the action with dash and spirit, so Montrose cried out: 'MacDonald drives all before him! Is his Clan to have all the honours this day?'

It was enough to send Gordon's horse charging from cover, screaming a war cry as they flung themselves down the slope and into the flank of Hurry's advancing troops. The Moray horse, still disordered after negotiating a bog, was so shocked by this sudden and unexpected attack that their commander, Drummond, gave the wrong word of command and, instead of wheeling round to present a front to the new attack, the horsemen wheeled left to override some of their own infantry, while offering their backs to the hotly pursuing Gordons, who emptied many a saddle in the chase. Aboyne, with the rest of the cavalry, had swung in against the flank and rear of the infantry attacking MacDonald and was making great inroads through their closely packed ranks. The Gordon foot broke from their left flank cover on Castle Hill and, in a steady disciplined mass, swept down upon Hurry's four infantry regiments, as, among the enclosures and pigsties, Alastair MacDonald rallied his Irishmen and charged into the enemy's reeling centre.

Ferociously assailed in front, flank and rear, the four regiments fought gallantly, but with the Northern Levies on their left rear, the cavalry reserve, and Sutherland's and Seaforth's men fleeing without striking a blow, the Covenanter army degenerated into a mob and fled the field. They were hotly pursued for fourteen miles, leaving behind 2,000 dead on the field as Hurry made his escape with less than 100 horsemen.

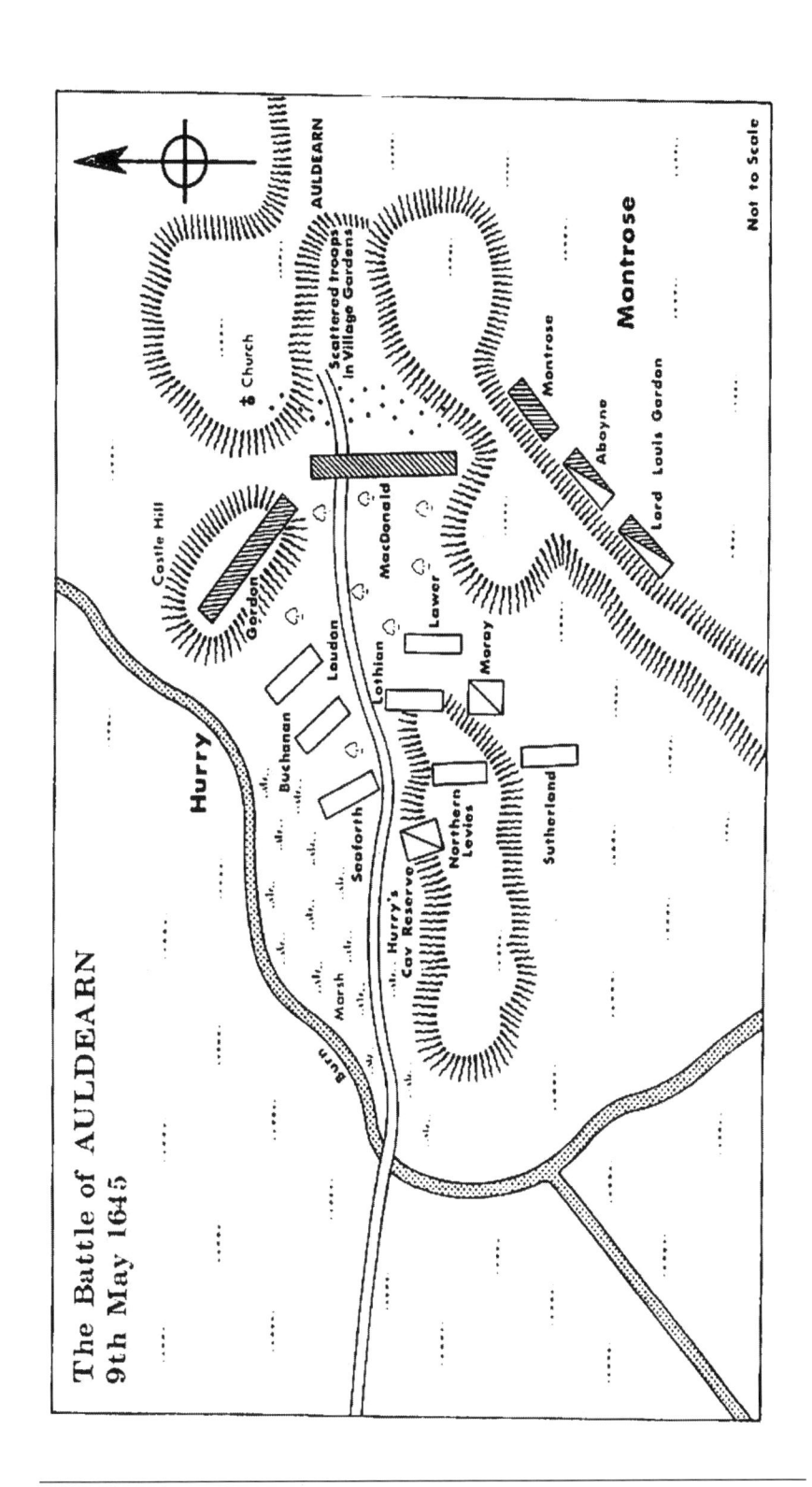

The Battle of AULDEARN
9th May 1645

## Reconstructing the Battle as a Wargame
Numbers are not important, provided there is a formation on the table to represent each of those historically present at this battle. The wargamer playing 'Montrose' should be told that he is about to be attacked, and be informed of the original tactics of that gifted Scottish commander. The wargamer representing Hurry should be allowed to believe that he is attacking a defensive position held by a much inferior force. The reconstruction begins with MacDonald, with his Irish troops and the Gordons, in position and Hurry beginning to move forward to the attack in the way he did historically.

The essential surprise factor is achieved by having the ridge on Montrose's left flank, behind which he hid his outflanking force, just on the table (as on the map), so that the outflanking force is 'off-table', ready to come on when 'Montrose' thinks fit to loose his attack.

Although there is a great numerical disparity between the forces plus a high element of surprise, it is not necessary to 'weight' the rules. The quality of the troops, assisted by such mêlée bonuses as those earned by Montrose's outflanking force for (1) a flank attack, (2) a downhill attack, and (3) complete surprise, should be sufficient to bring about the historical result.

At a vital stage of the battle Drummond gave the wrong command to the Moray Horse, so that his men turned away from the battle and were hit in rear. As this actually occurred, there must be a major chance of it also taking place in this wargame — by using percentage dice that allow Drummond only a 25 per cent chance of giving the correct order.

## Classification of Commanders
Montrose is just about as 'above average' as any commander in this book. On the day the same high rating must be given to MacDonald, Gordon and Aboyne. Hurry, the commander of the Covenanters, must be classified as 'below average' (1) for the natural reason that he did not show up well, and (2), from a practical point of view, to assist in balancing the disparity in numbers.

## Quality of Troops
On Montrose's side, the Irish regiments and the Gordon foot should be given an 'elite' rating, without which it is doubtful whether they will be able to contain the superior numbers facing them; and they must hold off the Covenanters long enough for Montrose to launch his outflanking cavalry. Montrose's cavalry, and the rest of his infantry, can be given an 'average' classification, although it might be thought fit (in view of the smallness of their numbers) to classify Gordon's and Aboyne's cavalry as 'elite'.

More the victims of misfortune and an ineffective commander on the day, the English regular infantry should be classified as 'average'. The Northern Levies and Hurry's cavalry reserve, and Sutherland's and Seaforth's men, all of whom broke and ran without taking part in the battle, are 'below average'. If the Moray horse are given the wrong order (according to the dice) and turn away, they should be 'below average', but should the dice favour them and they turn the right way, they can be classified as 'average'.

## Morale
The Royal army's morale was first-class, and appropriate bonuses should be given to the 'elite' troops. Hurry's men may all start off as first-class, although 'below average' troops could be given a second-class rating. Battle eventualities will cause fluctuations in morale and, if any 'weighting' is to be done, it can lower morale for Hurry's force when surprised during the battle.

## Effect and Construction of Terrain
As Montrose's keen tactical eye soon detected, this terrain was all important, possessing as it did good defensive positions for the small defending force and a made-to-measure place of concealment for outflanking troops. Similarly, the narrow front prevented the Covenanters taking advantage of their superiority in numbers.

It is not difficult to construct this terrain, using shaped blocks under a cloth or even stepped hills, though the wargamer should be careful about the positioning of important features of the landscape. The enclosures and pigsties can be represented by small stone walls running irregularly and interspersed with numerous gaps.

## Military Possibilities
The whole battle hinged on Hurry achieving surprise in his dawn attack, and had he not been so confident that his much larger army had achieved surprise, he might have used his artillery to soften up the enemy before attacking them. On the other hand, believing that he had Montrose's small army at his mercy, it is quite understandable that he should throw his forces into an immediate attack. If he had sat back, bombarded the position and perhaps permitted Montrose's men to escape by some back route, or if they had still managed to hold him off, history would have dealt hardly with Hurry. In any event, had Hurry used his artillery on MacDonald's Irish and Gordons, there is no doubt that this impetuous commander would have thrown his men forward in a wild attack upon the guns and perhaps captured them all early in the battle.

Montrose inspired the small and inexperienced cavalry force led by Gordon and Aboyne so that they plunged into the fray with great vigour, but had he not done so, their attack might well have failed. If Hurry's regular infantry had been given time to face them and put up a defensive front, it is quite likely that the Scots horsemen would have suffered the same fate as their fellow countrymen at Culloden one hundred years later — or they might have been sufficiently discouraged to attack only half-heartedly, and been thrust back.

If the Moray horse and Hurry's cavalry reserve, which together must have outnumbered Montrose's cavalry by at least two to one, had gathered and counterattacked, it is likely that they would have won the resulting mêlée. Not only would Montrose's horse have been outnumbered and possibly hit in flank, but the regular infantry facing them would either have had time to face about and form up against them, or to rally during the course of the mêlée and put up a better resistance.

It was not really important how long MacDonald held, so long as the Covenanters' attention was distracted from the possibility of a flank attack. Spice can be added to this game by ruling that Montrose's cavalry attack cannot take place before a certain game-move, and that move can be calculated by working out the time necessary for Montrose to assess the situation and arouse the horsemen to the right degree of confidence. For this ploy to succeed, the Covenanter infantry must be held until the move is due.

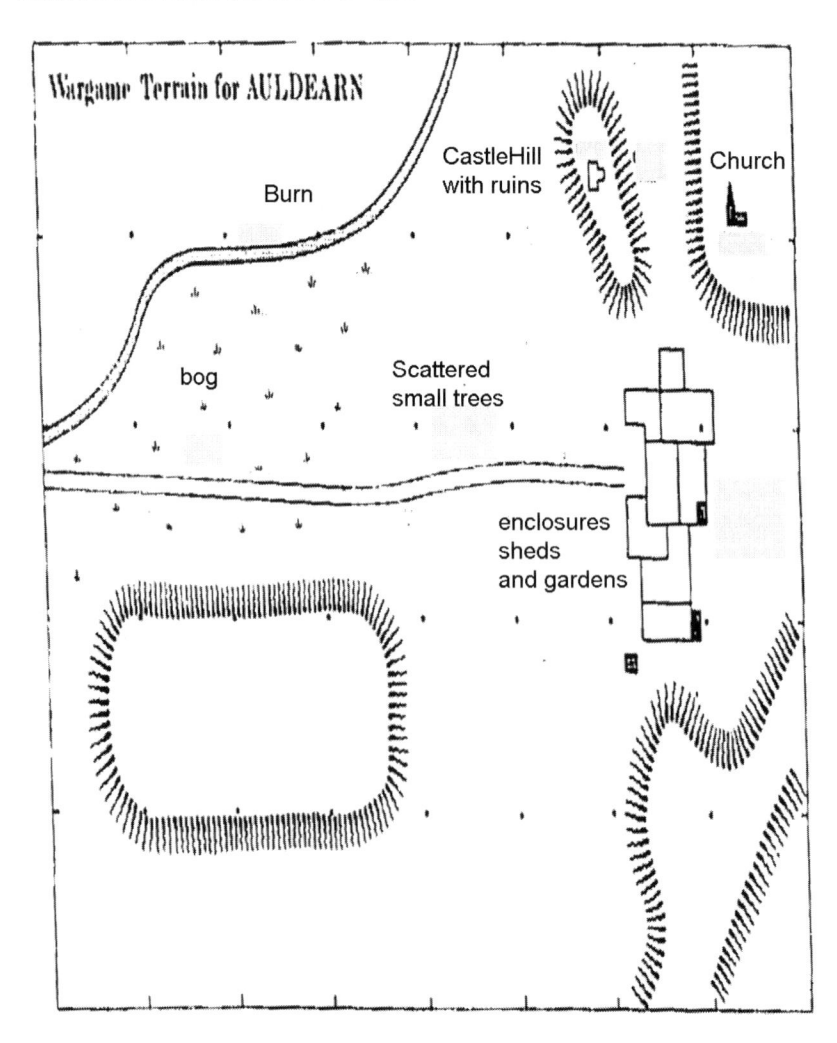

Wargame Terrain for AULDEARN

Burn

CastleHill with ruins

Church

bog

Scattered small trees

enclosures sheds and gardens

## 15. The Battle of the Dunes (Dunkirk) 14 June 1658

EARLY IN 1657, in a Treaty of Peace and Friendship with France, Oliver Cromwell agreed to provide 6,000 men, to be known as the Lord Protector's Forces and to be commanded by their own officers, plus a fleet of naval vessels for a campaign against the Spanish in Flanders. The object of the Treaty was to reduce the three coast towns of Mardyck, Dunkirk and Gravelines, and for England to take over the first two in pursuance of Cromwell's object of securing a Continental naval station to check any attempted invasion from Spanish Flanders by Charles Stuart. Although the English contingent included numerous old soldiers, it was largely made up of drafts and new recruits, formed into six regiments under Sir John Reynolds (lost at sea before this battle and replaced by Sir William Lockhart), with John Morgan, Monk's right-hand man in the Highland War, as Major-General.

There was some campaigning in 1657, when Mardyck was taken, and in spring 1658 Marshal Turenne, with the combined Franco-British army, laid siege to Spanish-held Dunkirk. A Spanish relieving force, marching so rapidly along the sandhills that it left its artillery behind, arrived near Zudcote within three miles of Dunkirk on 14 June and took up a position with its right on the sea, intending to await the arrival of the guns.

This Spanish army was a motley host some 15,000 strong under the joint commands of Don John of Austria; Conde, the French Catholic leader; the Marquis Caracena; and James, Duke of York (later to be James II of England). Stretching across the dunes, the army's right wing consisted of 6,000 Spanish infantry, with four of their regiments, under Caracena and Don John, on a sandhill, considered the key to the position. On the left of the Spanish the five British infantry regiments under the Duke of York were stationed, the King's Regiment of Foot Guards and Lord Muskerry's regiment (formed into one corps because of their small numbers) and the Duke of Gloucester's regiment in the first line, and Willoughby's regiment and Ormond's regiment (under Colonel Grace) in the second line. The centre and left-centre of the line was held by Germans, Walloons, Scots and Irish, while on the left wing was Conde with French and other infantry. The cavalry force was massed behind the foot in columns that stopped short of the beach, since they feared being fired on by the guns of the English fleet manoeuvring offshore.

The British regiments in the Spanish force consisted of some 2,000 men, three of them -- James's own (Muskerry's). Ormond's and the Duke of Gloucester's -- being Irish. Middleton's were Scots and the King's Regiment of Guards, made up mostly of refugees of 'gentle birth', were English.

Leaving 6,000 men guarding the siege-works, Turenne marched out at the head of 9,000 infantry, with 40 pieces of artillery. The force included six of Cromwell's regiments, the Scottish bodyguard of the Kings of France, the Regiment Douglas (at one time the Scottish brigade of King Gustavus Adolphus), and Dillon's Irish Regiment, which was made up of men who in fact had fled from the wrath of Cromwell. The Cromwellian-English were under the command of Sir William Lockhart and Morgan.

Turenne, one of the ablest generals of his time, formed up his army slowly and deliberately, coordinating his dispositions with the state of the tide, so that it was three hours before they were ready. The first line consisted of 13 troops of cavalry on the right wing, a similar number on the left and 11 battalions of infantry in the centre; the second line 10 troops of cavalry on the right, 9 on the left and 7 battalions of infantry in the centre. Five troops of horse were posted midway between the two lines of infantry and four more were held in reserve.

The Cromwellian English out-marched the French and were first into action, supported by the guns of their fleet firing upon the Spanish right. Covered by a cloud of skirmishers, their pikes advanced steadily to the foot of the sandhill while the musketeers wheeled right and left to maintain a steady fire as the pikes halted to regain their breath. Then, shouting at the top of their voices, they surged so impetuously up the treacherous sand slopes into the Spaniards and their supports, the English Foot Guards, that, although fighting well and hard, both Spanish and English were fairly swept off the hill to retire in confusion, leaving 7 out of 11 captains dead on the ground. James, Duke of York, tried to stop the rout by charging Lockhart's victorious regiment with his single troop of horse, but was beaten back; a second attempt broke into the infantry flank, but met such sturdy resistance that it too was pushed back. The remainder of the Cromwellian-English regiments advanced quickly in support and, with the help of the French left-wing cavalry of the Marquis de Castelnau, completed the rout of the Spanish right wing.

Its seaward flank uncovered, the whole of Don John's line, now engaged by the French infantry, wavered and fell back, until the Walloon and German infantry were in full retreat, taking their 'rearward' cavalry with them. On the right of the Walloons, the regiments of the Dukes of York and Gloucester held on a little longer, but at last they broke and fled, together with all the English contingent but the Foot Guards. Standing firm as on their left they were passed by the first line of the French infantry and on their right by some of Cromwell's regiments, they faced the second line of French, who called for their surrender. Then believing that they were the sole survivors of their army, they surrendered on advantageous terms.

On the extreme left of the Spanish line, Conde first successfully resisted the attacks of the French right wing, and his cavalry made a charge against the Marquis de Crequi that was only foiled by Turenne bringing cavalry from the French left wing, where they were unable to operate because of the incoming tide. Turenne's strategy of using the change of tide to enable him to carry out this cavalry envelopment of the Spanish left flank was a skilful use of local conditions. Ultimately Conde with all his troops were driven from the field, and the battle, which lasted from 8am to noon, ended in a complete victory for Turenne, with the loss of only about 400 men, mainly from the Cromwellian-English regiments. The Spanish lost 1,000 killed (their tercios were virtually annihilated) and 5,000 prisoners. Turenne pursued vigorously until nightfall, and the town of Dunkirk surrendered ten days later.

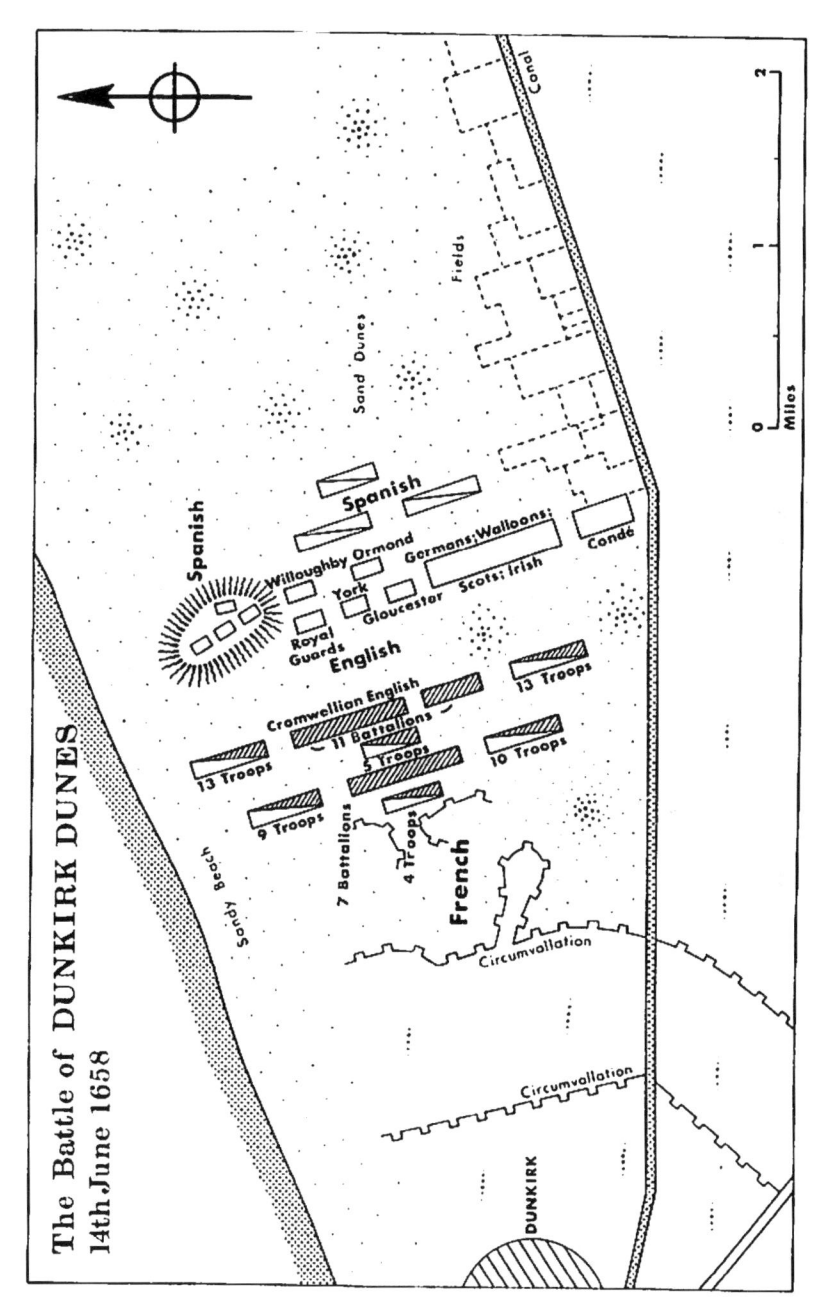

A notable omission in every report and on available maps of this battle is any trace of Turenne's 40 pieces of artillery or indeed of their use. Perhaps the Spanish army's complete lack of guns caused the French Marshal to scorn employing his immense superiority in this field, or maybe the lengthy artillery deployment period made his troops so impatient that they stormed forward without waiting for artillery support, thereby masking their own guns.

**Reconstructing the Battle as a Wargame**
The two armies form up in their historical dispositions. The French army could come on to the field in a strict order of march instead of in linear formation along their baseline, but this would give the Spanish a chance to attack them during the three hours it took for them to assemble. Such an attack would have no historical precedent, and would have to be made by troops, since the Spanish had no artillery.

The cavalry force covering Turenne's left flank did nothing at first, but its presence was tactically imperative until that wing received the protection of the incoming tide. Then Turenne was able to move his men across to swing the battle on the opposite wing. In any event, the seaward flank of Turenne's force was covered by the guns of the offshore fleet, which should be represented in this reconstruction as being 'off-table' but with its guns just within range of the beach. The tide will come in at a predetermined rate per game-move.

The Spanish considered their right wing to be the key position, and accordingly garrisoned it strongly. History indicates that Spanish troops were good, yet they were thrown off the hill in a relatively easy fashion. This could imply that they suffered a preliminary softening up by naval gunfire; in fact, to ensure that the Cromwellian-English attack is so quickly successful, it is best to lay down that the Spanish on the hill are initially bombarded from the sea.

**Classification of Commanders**
Turenne, the French commander, was 'above average'. Of the joint Spanish commanders, Don John, James, Duke of York, and Caracena were 'below average', but Conde, the veteran renegade French commander of the Spanish left wing, seems to have put up a better resistance and may be classified 'average' or perhaps 'above average'

**Quality of Troops and Morale**
The Cromwellian-English were 'elite' troops, but, to emphasise that superiority, their French comrades must be graded 'average'. With the exception of the English Fort Guards, which must be 'elite', the Spanish force cannot rate any higher classification than 'average'.

Throughout, the morale of the Cromwellian-English was first-class, like that of the French infantry and cavalry fighting alongside them. The Spanish infantry and their associated allies must be second-class, with the exception of the English Guards, who were first-class. As an alternative, the entire Spanish force can start off with first-class morale, which will fluctuate and descend according to circumstances. If this is done, the English Guards are given the rating of 'elite' troops, and add the agreed bonuses to all fighting qualities and morale.

### Effect and Construction of Terrain
The battlefield terrain does not seem to have had any effect upon the course of the battle; even the large hill occupied by the Spaniards was of no help to them. The undulating sand dunes undoubtedly made for heavy going but, as it was the same for everyone, movement distances should not be affected. Alternatively, fatigue penalties as described for Coutras can progressively affect everyone.

This is an easy terrain to construct. It may be made to undulate by draping a cloth over blocks of wood, books or other shapes dotted on the table top, with special emphasis on the large hill on the Spanish right.

### Military Possibilities
It is tempting to wonder whether the battle might have taken a different course if the Spanish artillery had been present, but then Turenne would surely have employed his 40 guns. If he had used them, and the Spanish were still without theirs, his victory would probably have been even easier. It is possible that the attack of the Cromwellian-English would not have been so overwhelmingly successful if the guns of the fleet had not softened up the Spaniards on the hill.

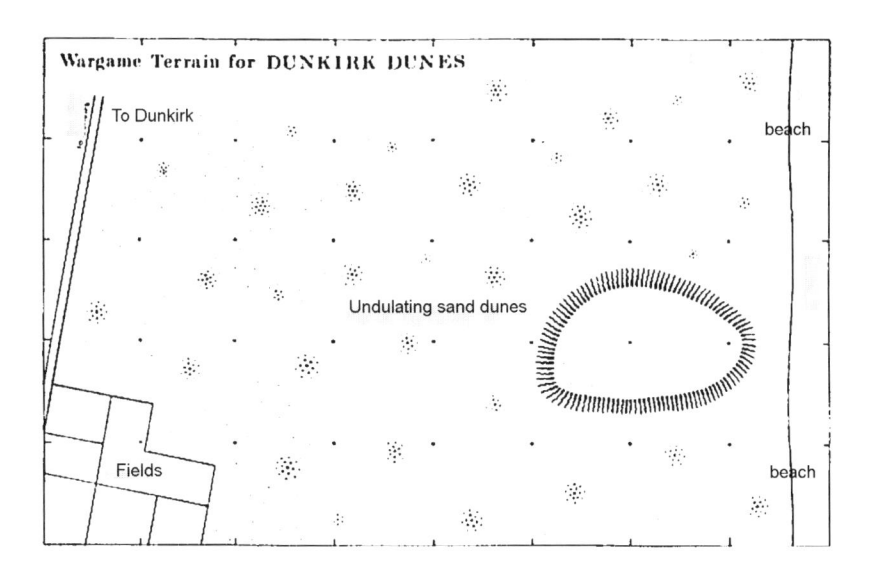

**Wargame Terrain for DUNKIRK DUNES**

# 16. English Civil War Rules by Donald Featherstone

*Supplemented by the reminiscences of Michael Curry*

These rules are intended to represent the grand tactical actions of the English Civil War. They represent the battle at an individual figure level with each figure representing 20 people. An inch = approximately 10 paces.

**Army Organisation**

Armies may have 1 to 3 generals depending on the size of the battle. Players should have approximately 6 to 8 units per general.

Units should be between 5 and 20 figures. Cannons are manned by 3-4 figures and represent 2-3 guns each.

**Sequence of Play**

Attacker in scenario moves first (or the highest roll on a die).

Player 1 selects a General to attempt to motivate units to move/ fire/ mêlée
Player 2 selects a general to attempt to motivate units etc.
Player 1 selects a general, and so on.

This continues until all generals on each side have had the chance to attempt to motivate units under their command.

Each general rolls to attempt to motivate one unit under his command. This continues until he fails to motivate a unit or every unit he commands has been motivated this turn. Then the initiative switches to the other side.

Motivation *is required for a unit to move/ fire/ mêlée*

The General rolls 2 dice, requires a score of 4 or above to activate unit.
+1 for every 6 inches from general
+1 if no line of sight
+1 enemy are between the direct line between general and unit
+1 unit took casualties last turn.
+1 general on hill, -1 general on foot

A unit is always motivated if a 9 or above is rolled.
No motivation roll is required for the general.

When unit is motivated roll 1 D6 per unit for movement points

## Movement point cost[8]

| | |
|---|---|
| 2 | One move (cavalry with pistols may fire, a unit may move into contact with the enemy without charging) (maximum of two moves in one turn) |
| 1 | Cross obstacle |
| 3 | limber/ unlimber guns |
| 1 | movement points to wheel (unless unit in column) |
| 1 | change formation |
| 3 | To change formation into/ out of pike block |
| 1 | Charge to contact (must have spent 2 points to move. |
| 2 | Fire muskets (maximum twice in one turn) |
| 3 | Artillery to fire +1 movement point per crew less than 4 |

Formations
Units may be in straight line/ column/ line or following a natural feature e.g. a hedge[9].

## Standard Movement Distances (inches)

```
Pike Block[10]                  4
Musket/ swordsmen/ pikes        5
Cavalry                         8
Cannon         Limbered         6
               Unlimbered       2
           Galloper Gun         8
General        mounted         15
               foot             7
Unit in column                + 2
```

*units may be moved twice in one turn if sufficient movement points have been rolled*

## Charge Rules

Units cannot change formation in a charge move.

---

[8] A modern wargamer would call these 'activation points'. Movement points was probably a concept borrowed from SPI boardgames at the time.

[9] E.g. a foot unit could be positioned along a wavy hedge line

[10] Pikes could be in loose formations e.g. a single line, but to be their most effective, they must be in a pike block, which then moves slowly and is more vulnerable to artillery (as it is a dense target).

Cavalry charging cavalry. Roll 4, 5 or 6 for enemy cavalry to counter charge (they may move forward up to 6 inches to meet charging unit).

**Firing**

Muskets roll a 10 sided decimal die, 2 ranks may fire.

|  |  | To hit roll |
|---|---|---|
| Muskets/ dragons | Short Range 0 - 5 inches | 9-10 |
| Muskets | Long Range 5+ – 10 inches | 10 |
| Cavalry pistol | 0 - 4 inches | 10 |

Modifiers

    1$^{st}$ time firing with muskets (1$^{st}$ Salvee) + 2 to hit
    Target in cover/ target gun crew -1
    Target moved into range last move –1
    Target in fortification –2
    Target pike block/ in column + 1

Cannon      long range is 20-30 inches

Roll a die for effect
    4 -5    1 casualty
    6      2 casualties

    Modifiers
        -1 target cannon crew
        -1 long range
        -1 target in hard cover
        + 1 target is pike block

## Mêlée adjacent figures each side rolls D10

|  |  | Defending figure |  |  |  |
|---|---|---|---|---|---|
|  |  | Musket/ pikes | Pike block | Cavalry | Cannon crew |
| Attacking figure | Musket/ pikes | 9,10 | 10 | 10 | 8-10 |
|  | Pike block | 6-10 | 9-10 | 7-10 | 7-10 |
|  | Cannon crew | 10 | 10 | 10 | 9-10 |
|  | Cavalry | 8-10 | 10 | 9-10 | 6-10 |

Save rolls apply to casualties

Modifiers
Attacker
+1 Charged to combat
+1 Flank attack
+ 2 attacking rear
+1 defending obstacle
+1 direct support (defined as friendly figure behind figure in mêlée)

Defender
+1 behind obstacle

Side with most casualties is forced back 2 inches

Cavalry automatically follow up a unit they are mêléeing that is forced back; to try to rally and reform to prevent this roll a D10.
Royalist           1 - 4
Parliamentary      1 - 6

## Morale

4 figures is the minimum unit size. Units smaller than this flee the battlefield and are removed.

An army routs when more than 50% of its units have routed.

# Appendix 1 Rules for Wargames[11]

THE LITTLE metal and plastic soldiers used in wargaming are not endowed with any personal fighting qualities or morale, and these essential military attributes have to be bestowed upon them. The battles in this book were for the most part fought by professional soldiers with a sprinkling of hardened, if slightly unreliable, mercenaries. Some soldiers were better than others — the Swedes of Gustavus Adolphus and the Swiss pikemen, for instance, were outstanding warriors — and if authenticity is to prevail upon the wargames table, soldiers' abilities must be reflected in a practical manner. The detrimental influence of the poorer commander must also be reflected, for almost without exception, each of our battles is marked by one commander being markedly inferior to his opposite number. Other factors to consider are numerical disparity of forces, surprise, superiority of weapons (such as the light regimental guns of the Swedes), and differing morale states. All must be simulated and controlled by rules compiled upon a sound historical basis.

Wargaming rules are based on knowledge of the specific period, backed by the experience and intentions of the wargamers themselves. The first intention is to produce the greatest possible realism, enabling period tactics and fighting qualities to be authentically simulated.

Amateur rulemakers may study the period they are attempting to return to before putting pen to paper, but even then no two sets of rules are likely to agree, since each will embody much of the character and temperament of their devisor. For instance, a person unaccustomed to horses may produce a set of rules giving undue weight to the effects of cavalry charges, or a person with a cool head may undervalue the effect of surprise. Frankly, rules are nearly all theory in the sense that few wargamers[12] have heard a shot fired in anger, their impressions of warfare having been acquired from the books they read. Hence, rules vary enormously.

Such variations can be avoided by using some of the better commercially produced rules and, so far as this period is concerned, there is a club devoted entirely to it. The Pike-and-Shot Society[13] issues a bimonthly magazine called *The Arquebusier*, and publishes a set of excellent rules.

---

[11] A list of currently available rules for the period has been added to this appendix.

[12] Notable exceptions are Georg von Reisswitz, author of the Prussian military training game, *Kriegsspiel*, first published in 1824, who served in 1813-14; Brigadier Peter Young, author of *Charge!* who served in the Commandos in World War II, and – of course – Donald Featherstone himself!

[13] Contact the P&SS at http://www.pikeandshotsociety.org/index.htm

No set of rules can cover all battlefield eventualities: for example, few known sets of rules lacking 'local' amendments would give victory to the young Enghien at Rocroi by allowing any chance of success for his charge through the centre of the Spanish infantry formation. This is one of those extraordinary historical situations beyond conventional wargame rules, which are formulated for the wargaming norm. In fact, Enghien at Rocroi could be given a 25 per cent chance of bringing off his courageous but foolhardy attack by the use of a pair of percentage dice, which would reveal whether the young French leader can reproduce his astonishing feat on the wargames table. Exceptional incidents, which frequently crop up in battles of all periods, may also be handled by 'local' rules, or by 'weighting' a rule to make them possible.

Rules supply order where anarchy would otherwise prevail. As wargaming presents opportunities for acrimony, games must be controlled by rules that are both fair and historically accurate.

## SOME WARGAME RULES FOR THE PIKE-AND-SHOT PERIOD
In addition to the rules given in this book, readers may wish to look at these:

*1644: Rules for Battles of the English Civil War,* Rick Priestley, Foundry
  Publications, http://wargamesfoundry.com

A *Battle of Dreux* scenario may be found on the internet at:
  www.rebelpublishing.net/pdfs/The_Battle_of_Dreux.pdf

*Father Tilly* [Thirty Year's War tactical rules], Stephen Danes, may be
  purchased as pdfs from www.sabersedge.com/stephendanes.php

*Field of Glory Renaissance,* Richard Bodley Scott, Osprey/Slitherine,
  www.ospreypublishing.com

*Impetus:game rules for miniature battles* [tactical rules for Ancient, Medieval
  and Renaissance periods], Dadi & Piombo; the free to download
*Basic*
  *Baroque* expansion has rules and army lists for the Eighty Years'
  War/Dutch Revolt, Thirty Years' War and English Civil Wars. Website:
  www.dadiepiombo.com/impetus2.html

*Pike and Plunder: A Wargames Campaign for the Italian Wars,* James
  Roach, available for purchase from Vexillia Limited at:
  http://pikeandplunder.vexillia.ltd.uk

*Pike and Shot English Civil War Wargame Rules*, John Armatys, free to

download at:
www.wargamedevelopments.org/game_downloads/Pands.pdf

*Polemos English Civil War* [tactical rules for larger battles], Peter Berry, may
   be purchased as hard copy or pdf from: www.baccus6mm.com

*Regiment of Foote* [ECW tactical], Peter Pig Rules For the Common Man,
   may be purchased from: www.peterpig.co.uk

*Spanish Fury: Battle* [tactical rules for 16$^{th}$ century], The Perfect Captain
   website. See also the *Actions!* [small unit/skirmishes] and *Campaign*
   modules at: http://perfectcaptain.50megs.com/SpanishMain.html

*Tinker Fox* [ECW campaign system], The Perfect Captain website at:
   http://perfectcaptain.50megs.com/tfox.html

*Very Civile Actions* [ECW tactical rules], The Perfect Captain website at:
   http://perfectcaptain.50megs.com/vcactions.html

*Wargames Campaigns* [campaign and simple tactical rules in ECW Battle of
   Alton Church scenario], D. F. Featherstone (1970)

*Wargames Through the Ages,* Vol. II, *1420-1783,* D. F. Featherstone (1974)

*Wargaming: An Introduction* [contains simple Pike and Shot period rules],
   Neil Thomas, The History Press Ltd

*Wargaming Pike and Shot*, Charlie Wesencraft, History of Wargaming
   Project

*Warhammer English Civil War,* John Stallard, may be purchased from:
   http://www.warhammer-historical.com/index.html

See also the websites:

http://www.freewargamesrules.co.uk/
http://www.miniaturewargaming.com/
http://www.juniorgeneral.org/

for a wide variety of free rules for this period; Matt Fritz's Junior General website also has scenarios for some ECW battles and printable paper soldiers.

# Appendix 2 Availability of Wargames Figures[14]

IN THIS day and age the wargamer has at his disposal an extensive choice of commercially produced wargames figures, in a variety of scales and for every conceivable period. The formation of the Pike-and-Shot Society[15] undoubtedly stimulated manufacturers to increase and improve their range of figures for the period, and it is now possible to obtain commercial figures for each and every army mentioned in this book. The only limitations are those of finance, for 25/28mm metal figures cost approximately 30-50p per figure, with cavalry about double. Smaller figures such as the 6mm, 10mm and 15mm ranges are cheaper, but may not be to everyone's taste.

The constantly increasing ranges of 20mm soft plastic figures manufactured originally by Airfix, but now also by numerous American and European companies, have the merit of covering many periods of history and of being easily convertible to any desired soldier of any period. This invaluable fact puts universal wargaming within the reach of even the schoolboy with limited financial resources. Recently, some companies have started producing wargame figures in hard polystyrene, which are even easier to convert. For instructions on converting plastic figures read Chapter 5 of *Military Modelling* by D. F. Featherstone (Kaye and Ward, 1970).

Manufacturers make model soldiers for wargames in the following scales: 2mm troop blocks, 1/300 or 6mm, 10mm, 15mm, 20mm and 25/28mm individual figures. Scales do not necessarily fit in with each other, and the so-called 25mm figure of one manufacturer may appear minute beside the 25mm figure of another. It is essential to check figure sizes before buying from different manufacturers, or one's soldiers will vary from dwarfs to giants!

The names and website addresses listed below are some of the principal makers of lead and plastic wargames figures at the present time. All their products are good, and the wargamer will soon decide for himself which he prefers.

**SOME WARGAME FIGURES FOR THE PIKE-AND-SHOT PERIOD**
(Listed by size/scale)
**2mm**

---

[14] This section has been updated to reflect the availability of wargame figures for this period in 2010. Only figures manufactured, or easily obtained, in the United Kingdom are listed.

[15] The P&SS publishes a bi-monthly 40 page A5 journal, *The Arquebusier*, available from http://www.pikeandshotsociety.org/index.htm and has an internet discussion group at http://groups.yahoo.com/group/PikeandShotSociety/

Irregular Miniatures ( www.irregularminiatures.co.uk ) have a Renaissance range containing figures suitable for the Italian Wars, the Thirty Years' War and the English Civil Wars

**6mm or 1/300 scale**

Baccus ( www.baccus6mm.com ) has an extensive English Civil War range. The website also has information on uniforms and colours.

Heroics and Ros www.heroicsandros.co.uk has a small Renaissance range suitable for the Italian Wars and a somewhat larger range for the English Civil Wars.

Irregular Miniatures ( www.irregularminiatures.co.uk ) have an Italian Wars range, and a Late Renaissance range suitable for the Fall of Hungary, the French Wars of Religion, the Dutch Revolt, the Thirty Years' War and the English Civil Wars.

**10/12mm**

Miniature Figurines (http://miniaturefigurines.co.uk/Home.aspx ), now owned by Caliver Books of Nottingham has a 12mm English Civil War range.

Old Glory UK Grand Scale (www.oldgloryuk.com ) has an English Civil War range.

Pendraken (www.pendraken.co.uk ) has Landsknechts, early 16th century English and Scots, 16th century Ottomans and Poles, Thirty Years' War and English Civil Wars ranges.

**15mm**

Essex Miniatures ( www.essexminiatures.co.uk ) has a Renaissance range containing Landsknechts, Muscovites, Poles, Turks, the Thirty Years' War and the English Civil Wars.

FreiKorp 15 ( http://quickreactionforce.co.uk/ ) has ranges suitable for the Italian Wars, Tudor Wars, Elizabeth's Irish Wars, the Thirty Years' War, the English Civil Wars and Renaissance Turks.

Irregular Miniatures ( www.irregularminiatures.co.uk ) have a Renaissance 1600-1700 range suitable for the Thirty Years' War and the English Civil Wars.

Matchlock Miniatures, owned by Caliver Books of Nottingham (http://www.wargames.co.uk/traders/caliver/matchlock.htm ) has a Pike & Shot range covering the Italian Wars, the Thirty Years' War and the English Civil Wars. The latter range includes characters such as Puritan preachers, witchfinders and a wounded man being treated by a surgeon.

Miniature Figurines (http://miniaturefigurines.co.uk/Home.aspx ) has figures suitable for the Italian Wars, the French Wars of Religion, the Dutch Revolt, the Fall of Hungary and the English Civil Wars.

Peter Pig ( www.peterpig.co.uk ) has an English Civil War range.

## 20mm

When this book was originally published, Airfix was the only manufacturer of soft plastic 20mm toy historical military figures, but never produced figures for this period, so early wargamers expended much ingenuity and time in converting them. Today the number of American and European manufacturers of such figures is too great to list them all here; instead, readers are recommended to visit the very useful website http://www.plasticsoldierreview.com/Index.aspx where they will find listings by historical period, detailed reviews of accuracy and poses and photographs.

Irregular Miniatures ( www.irregularminiatures.co.uk ) have Renaissance figures for Muscovites, Poles and Turks only. Swiss pikemen may be found in their Late Medieval range.

## 25/28mm

Essex Miniatures ( www.essexminiatures.co.uk ) has a Renaissance range containing late 16th century Spanish troops, Muscovites, Poles, Turks, the Thirty Years' War and the English Civil Wars.

Foundry Miniatures (http://wargamesfoundry.com/ ) have Medieval Swiss pikemen and handgunners, Renaissance French and Germans suitable for the Italian Wars; English and Spanish troops of the late 16th century suitable for the Dutch Revolt, and an extensive English Civil Wars range – which includes German troops for the Thirty Years War.

Irregular Miniatures ( www.irregularminiatures.co.uk ) Renaissance range contains figures for all the campaigns covered in this book.

Matchlock Miniatures, owned by Caliver Books of Nottingham (http://www.wargames.co.uk/traders/caliver/matchlock.htm ) has a Pike & Shot range which covers the Italian Wars and the English Civil Wars.

Miniature Figurines (http://miniaturefigurines.co.uk/Home.aspx ) has a Renaissance range with a selection of figures suitable for the 16th century and separate ranges for the Thirty Years' War and the English Civil War.

Old Glory (www.oldgloryuk.com ) has ranges for the Italian Wars, the Wars of Religion, the Fall of Hungary and the English Civil Wars.

Perry Miniatures (http://www.perry-miniatures.com/ ) has a range of metal figures for the English Civil Wars.

Warlord Games ([www.warlordgames.co.uk/](www.warlordgames.co.uk/) ) has a growing Pike & Shotte range of metal and hard plastic figures for the Thirty Years' War and English Civil Wars.

# Appendix 3 Terrain

WHEN RECONSTRUCTING a historical battle, be sure the topographical features and the dimensions of the terrain bear the closest affinity to the historical field, or what occurs upon it will bear only the most coincidental resemblance to those military activities that are being simulated. Each of the engagements under review has not only been chosen because of its suitability for reconstruction but also because it was fought on a terrain that is reasonable to construct on an average 8 feet by 5 feet wargames table. The terrain maps have also been drawn to this scale.

It is strongly urged that completed wargames terrains should only include those parts of the field over which fighting actually occurred, or those parts which have an integral bearing on the realistic simulation of the battle. Otherwise, all the model soldiers will be crowded into perhaps half the table.

The battles notably influenced by their terrain are Coutras, Dreux, Arques, Nieuport (in the sense of its tiring effect upon the combatants), Cropredy Bridge and Auldearn. If their reconstruction is to be accurate and successful, these terrains should be measured and constructed with care. The remainder are simple and will take only minutes to put together.

The easiest manner of constructing a wargames terrain to produce the undulating surface of so many fields is to stretch a green cloth or suitably coloured plastic sheet over mounds of books, slabs of expanded polystyrene from packaging or pieces of wood placed in suitable positions on the table top. Even though it may mean 'ironing out' the known contours of the battlefield, hills and slopes must possess gradients no greater than will allow model soldiers to stand up on them. Slabs of wood or expanded polystyrene tiles placed upon each other and covered will form stepped hills which, though giving the terrain a symbolic appearance, will provide readily definable contours and good surfaces for model soldiers to stand on. Strips of suitably coloured cloth, paper or self-adhesive sheets can be stuck on to form rivers and roads, or these features may be painted directly onto the plastic sheet with poster paint.

Undoubtedly the most realistic wargames terrain is that constructed on a sand table, and moulded into hills, valleys, sunken roads, river beds, trenches etc. But sand tables are few and far between and present considerable difficulties. They are discussed in some detail in the book *Wargames* and the booklet *Wargames Terrain* (published by the author).

Few stretches of land are quite bare of vegetation, and the appearance of any battlefield is greatly improved by scaled-down clumps of trees, bushes and scrub. As wargames-table woods and clearings have to be accessible to model soldiers (who may be fitted three or four to a stand), they must be so constructed that space is allowed for such manoeuvres. This can be achieved by shaping a piece of hardboard to represent the area of the wood, painting it a darker colour than the table top upon which it stands, and fixing a few toy trees round its edge. Trees and hedges can be made from lichen moss stuck on twigs, or bought ready-made from model railway and hobby shops; stone walls, bridges and rail fencing can be made from balsa wood or similarly purchased; broken pieces of polystyrene, painted grey, make ideal crags and rocky outcrops.

Plastic and card kits of houses are readily obtainable[16], or buildings can be made from cardboard or represented by blocks of wood. It is never easy conveniently to arrange troops within the houses they are defending, but one simple method of dealing with the problem is to remove from the table the number of troops claimed to be in a particular house, mark the number on a small V-shaped ticket, and lay that across the ridge of the rooftop. As casualties reduce the number of men so represented, other tickets can be used or the original number erased and the new one substituted.

There is a deplorable tendency among wargamers to lavish most of their time and attention on model soldiers and only a minimum upon the table-top terrains over which they fight[17]. As enjoyment of a wargame can vary in relation to the degree of realism of the miniature battlefield, care should be taken to ensure that it presents a pleasing and authentic appearance. The battles in this book, if fought by the means suggested, should closely resemble their historical counterparts. Even if history is ignored, as long as the terrain is realistic the wargame will at least bear some resemblance to the real battle.

---

[16] The suppliers of model railway buildings, scenery and accessories are excellent sources for creating wargame battlefield terrain. See, for example, the Howard Scenic Supplies website: http://www.howardscenicsupplies.co.uk/

[17] Although today some 'old school' wargamers favour the stylised, minimalist terrain shown in early wargame books such as *Little Wars* or *Charge!*, others construct diorama-standard battlefields for their games, as shown in the pages of *Wargames Illustrated* and *Miniature Wargaming*.

# Bibliography[18]

THE FOLLOWING books were used in preparing this volume. Besides providing information for the specific battles listed below, almost all contain information about the arms and equipment, style of fighting and tactics of the armies of the period.

Barrett, C. B. R. *Battles and Battlefields in England* (1896). Cropredy Bridge
Birnic, Arthur. *The Art of War* (1942). Breitenfeld, Lutzen
Buchan, John. *Montrose* (1928). Auldearn
Chandler, David. *A Traveller's Guide to the Battlefields of Europe,* 2 vols (1965). Vol 1, Pinkie, Arques, Rocroi, Dunes; Vol 2, Pavia, Mohacs, Breitenfeld, Liitzen
—. *The Art of Warfare on Land* (1974). Nicuport, Breitenfeld, Lutzen
Coggins, Jack. *The Fighting Man* (1966). Lutzen
Dupuy, Ernest and Trevor. *The Encyclopaedia of Military History* (1970). All battles
Eggenberger, David. *A Dictionary of Battles* (1967). Ravenna, Pavia, Nieuport, Breitenfeld, Lutzen, Rocroi, Dunes
Falls, Cyril. *Great Military Battles* (1964). Rocroi
Featherstone, D. F. *Wargames Through the Ages,* Vol I, *3000 BC to AD 1500* (1972), Ravenna, Pavia, Mohacs, Ceresole, Pinkie, Dreux, Arques; Vol II, *1420-1783* (1974), Pavia, Ceresole, Coutras, Breitenfeld, Lutzen, Rocroi, Cropredy Bridge, Auldearn, Dunes
Fortescue, J. W. *History of the British Army,* Vol I (1899). Dunes
Geyl, P. *The Netherlands* War (1947). Nieuport
Grant, James. *British Battles on Land and Sea* (1890). Pinkie, Dunes
Green, Howard. *Guide to the Battlefields of Britain and Ireland* (1973). Pinkie, Cropredy Bridge
Hamilton, Sir F. W. *The Origin and History of the First or Grenadier Guards,* Vol I (1874). Dunes
Kinross, John. *Discovering Battlefields in Southern England* (1970). Cropredy Bridge
Montgomery, FM Viscount. *History of Warfare* (1968). Mohacs, Nieuport. Breitenfeld
Montluc, Blaise de. *The Hapsburg-Valois Wars and the French Wars of Religion* (reprinted 1972). Coutras, Dreux, Arques
Montross, Lynn. *War Through the Ages* (1944). Nieuport, Breitenfeld, Lutzen
Oman, Sir Charles. *A History of the Art of War in the Sixteenth Century* (1937). Ravenna, Pavia, Mohacs, Ceresole, Pinkie. Dreux, Coutras, Arques, Nieuport

---

[18] The original bibliography is reproduced first here, though many of the books listed are now out of print and only obtainable from secondhand or antiquarian book dealers or via inter-library loan. It is followed by a short list of more recently published books that may assist the reader who wishes to research any of the battles further.

Pratt, Fletcher. *The Battles That Changed History* (1956). Breitenfeld, Lutzen

Rogers, H. C. B. *Battles and Generals of the Civil Wars, 1612-1651*(1968). Auldearn

Taylor, F. L. *The Art of War in Italy, 1494-1529* (1921). Ravenna, Pavia, Ceresole

Thompson, J. W. *Wars of Religion in France, 15591576* (1958). Dreux, Coutras, Arques

Toynbee, Margaret and Young, Peter. *Cropredy Bridge, 1644: The Campaign and the Battle* (1970). Cropredy Bridge

Treece, Henry and Oakeshott, Ewart. *Fighting Men* (1963). Ravenna, Pavia, Ceresole, Pinkie, Dreux, Arques

Wedgwood. C. V. *The Thirty Years' War* (1938). Breitenfeld, Lutzen, Rocroi

Wood, Sir Evelyn. *British Battles on Land and Sea* (1915). Pinkie

The magazines *Wargamers' Newsletter*, *Slingshot* and *Tradition* also contributed much material of value.

These books are also recommended:

Boudet.J. *The Ancient Art of Warfare* (1969)

Fuller, J. F. C. *Decisive Battles of the Western World, 40 BC-1757* (1954)

Halevy, D. *Armies and Their Arms* (1962)

Norman, A. V. B. and Pottinger, D. *Warrior to Soldier, 449-1660*(1966)

Oman, C. W. C. *The Art of War in the Middle Ages, AD 378-1515* (1953)

Perroy, E. *The Hundred Years War* (1951)

Weller.J. *Weapons and Tactics* (1966)

**SOME MORE RECENT BOOKS (listed by title in chronological order)**

**General**

*European Warfare 1494-1660,* Jeremy Black, Routledge Warfare in History
    Series

*Fighting Tactics of the Early Modern World AD 1500 – AD 1763: Equipment, Combat Skills and Tactics*, Christopher Jorgensen, Michael E. Pavkovic,
    Ron S. Rice, Frederick C. Schneid, Chris L. Scott, Spellmount, is
    particularly useful, as it contains full colour annotated battle diagrams of
    Nieuport, Breitenfeld and Lutzen

*A Guide to Battles: Decisive Conflicts in History,* edited by Richard Holmes
    and Martin Matrix Evans, Oxford Paperback Reference

*Matchlock Musketeer 1588-1688*, Keith Roberts, Osprey Warrior 48

*Pike and Shot Tactics 1590-1660*, Keith Roberts, Osprey Elite 179
*The Art of Renaissance Warfare from the Fall of Constantinople to the Thirty Years' War,* Stephen Turnbull, Greenhill Books
*The Military Revolution: Military Innovation and the Rise of the West 1500-*
   *1800*, Geoffrey Parker, Cambridge University Press
*The Renaissance at War*, Thomas Arnold, Cassell's History of Warfare

### Italian Wars
*Condottiere 1300-1500*, David Murphy, Osprey Warrior 115
*Italian Medieval Armies 1300-1500*, David Nicolle, Osprey Men At Arms 136
*The Landsknechts*, Douglas Miller, Osprey Men At Arms 58
*Landsknecht Soldier 1486-1560*, John Harald Richards, Osprey Warrior 49
*Pavia 1525: The Climax of the Italian Wars*, Angus Konstam, Osprey
   Campaigns 44
*The Swiss at War 1300-1500*, Douglas Miller, Osprey Men At Arms 94

### The Ottomans
*Armies of the Ottoman Turks 1300-1774*, David Nicolle, Osprey Men At
   Arms 140
*Hungary and the Fall of Eastern Europe 1000-1568*, David Nicolle, Osprey
   Men At Arms 195
*The Janissaries*, David Nicolle, Osprey Elite 58
*The Ottoman Empire 1326-1699*, Stephen Turnbull, Osprey Essential
   History 62

### Tudor Warfare
*Henry VIII's Army*, Paul Cornish, Osprey Men At Arms 191
*Scottish Renaissance Armies 1513-1550*, Jonathan Cooper, Osprey Elite
   167
*Tudor Knight*, Christopher Gravett, Osprey Warrior 104

### French Religious Wars
*The French Religious Wars 1562-1598*, Robert Jean Knecht, Osprey
   Essential Histories 47
*The King's Army: Warfare, Soldiers and Society during the Wars of Religion
   in France, 1562-76*, James B. Wood, Cambridge Studies in Early Modern
   History

### The Dutch Revolt
*The Army of Flanders and the Spanish Road 1567-1659: The Logistics of*

*Spanish Victory and Defeat in the Low Countries' Wars,* Geoffrey Parker,
  Cambridge University Press
*The Dutch Revolt,* Geoffrey Parker, Penguin Books
*The Grand Strategy of Philip II,* Geoffrey Parker, Yale University Press

**Thirty Years' War**
*Army of Gustavus Adolphus 1: Infantry,* Richard Brzezinski, Osprey
*Army of Gustavus Adolphus 2: Cavalry,* Richard Brzezinski, Osprey
*Imperial Army of the Thirty Years' War 1: Infantry,* Vladimir Brnardic, Osprey
  Men At Arms 457
*Imperial Army of the Thirty Years' War 2: Cavalry,* Vladimir Brnardic, Osprey
  Men At Arms 462
*Lutzen1632: The Climax of the Thirty Years' War,* Richard Brzezinski,
  Osprey Campaigns 68
*The Thirty Years' War,* Richard Bonney, Osprey Essential History 299

**English Civil Wars**
*A Military History of the English Civil War: 1642-1649,* Malcolm Wanklyn and
  Frank Jones, Longman
*Auldearn 1645: the Marquis of Montrose's Scottish Campaign,* Stuart Reid,
  Osprey Campaigns 123
*Cromwell's War Machine: The New Model Army 1645-1660,* Keith Roberts,
  Pen and Sword
*Decisive Battles of the English Civil War,* Malcolm Wanklyn, Pen and Sword
*Scots Armies of the English Civil War,* Stuart Reid, Osprey Men At Arms 331
*Soldiers of the English Civil War 1: Infantry,* Keith Roberts, Osprey Elite 25
*Soldiers of the English Civil War 2: Cavalry,* John Tincey, Osprey Elite 27
*The English Civil Wars 1642-51,* Peter Gaunt, Osprey Essential History 58
*The English Civil War 1642-1651: An Illustrated Military History,* Philip
  Haythornthwaite, Blandford Press Ltd.
*English Civil War Artillery 1642-51,* Chris Henry, Osprey New Vanguard 108
*Ironsides: English Cavalry 1588-1688,* John Tincey, Osprey Warrior

Printed in Great Britain by
Amazon.co.uk, Ltd.,
Marston Gate.